3/5/14

Praise for *Decide*

"Steve's approach is not only hugely engaging but has an immediate impact on motivation and productivity. His book is the next best thing to having Steve in the room. I highly recommend it!"

—**Christina Harper Elgarresta**
Managing Director, Accenture

"*Decide* delivers: If you're struggling to lead, not just manage; if you're frustrated that your very best results are just beyond reach; or if you're simply at war with your calendar, Steve McClatchy's new book is for you. *Decide* is a rare fresh take at some of the thorny problems that block our best work. But don't just take my word for it. Get your own copy, and you'll soon be ordering copies for your team as well."

—**Marshall Goldsmith**
America's preeminent executive coach
(*Fast Company* magazine)

"*Decide* puts personal power squarely where it belongs—in your hands. Follow Steve's advice, and you'll immediately see benefits that will change the way you plan, spend your time, and engage with others. To change your trajectory and start leading in all aspects of your life, all you have to do is *decide*."

—**Mary Davis Holt**
Leadership coach, speaker, and best-selling
coauthor of *Break Your Own Rules*

"I have worked with Steve, and I can say firsthand that his approach has had a profound impact on every level of our organization. His methods are deeply insightful and tremendously impactful. I highly recommend Steve, his approach, and this book!"

—**Luc Robitaille**
President of Business Operations,
Los Angeles Kings Hockey Club

"In *Decide*, Steve McClatchy shows us that we can accomplish amazing things by aligning what we want to achieve with how we spend our time. Regardless of the industry or level of the reader, real benefits will be accomplished from Steve's advice—an immensely practical guide!"

—**Valerie Sutton**
Director of Career Services,
Harvard Graduate School of Education

"As the late Professor Randy Pausch said, 'It's not how long you live, rather how well you live.' *Decide* shows how we can all live more meaningful, productive lives simply by practicing better decision making. I invite you—and your team—to start regaining control over your time and efforts by reading this important book."

—**Navi Radjou**
Speaker, advisor, and best-selling author,
including author of *Jugaad Innovation* and
From Smart to Wise

"World-class leadership is about making inspired and enlightened choices. With fresh stories and advice, McClatchy drills down to this idea by recommending daily habits that leaders at every level can use to their immediate benefit. *Decide* is a very worthy read on a critical subject."

—**Douglas R. Conant**
Chairman of Avon Products, founder of Conant Leadership,
and *New York Times* best-selling
author of *TouchPoints*

"Your success as a leader is as good as your decisions. McClatchy shows you how to make the decisions every day that will keep your business and you moving forward."

—**Elizabeth Walker**
Vice President, Global Talent Management,
Campbell Soup Company

"If your intention is to gain from your life, and not just prevent the pain that often comes with it, then *Decide* is the book for you. Steve McClatchy reminds us that to achieve something of significance, we have to focus on things that matter. His new book is full of the practical wisdom that will enable you to end burnout and bring balance to your life—and to find a path worthy of being followed. I absolutely recommend this book."

—Jim Kouzes
Coauthor of *The Leadership Challenge* and
Executive Fellow of Leadership, Leavey School of Business,
Santa Clara University

decide

dec!de

work smarter,

reduce your stress,

and lead by example

Steve McClatchy

WILEY

Cover image and design: Paul McCarthy

Published by John Wiley & Sons, Inc., Hoboken, New Jersey.
Published simultaneously in Canada.

For general information about our other products and services, please contact our Customer
Care Department within the United States at (800) 762-2974, outside the United States at (317)
572-3993 or fax (317) 572-4002.

Wiley publishes in a variety of print and electronic formats and by print-on-demand. Some
material included with standard print versions of this book may not be included in e-books or in
print-on-demand. If this book refers to media such as a CD or DVD that is not included in the
version you purchased, you may download this material at http://booksupport.wiley.com. For
more information about Wiley products, visit www.wiley.com.

ISBN: 978-1-118-55438-8 (cloth)
ISBN: 978-1-118-77165-5 (ebk)
ISBN: 978-1-118-77167-9 (ebk)

Printed in the United States of America

10 9 8 7 6 5 4 3 2 1

To Lynn, Grace, Amy, Kyle, and Kelly,
for being the reason that I work hard, rush home, and smile.
Thank you for your confidence and trust,
your support, and your abundant love.
This book is for you.

Contents

Preface

The material in this book has been presented to high-level executives as well as high school and college students and people in every stage of life in between, over the past 12 years. It is a message of leadership that everyone can relate to in their own way because everyone has the opportunity to be a leader, whether it's for a team of professionals or in their own lives.

Decide aims to help readers lead toward improvement in their business and their life by teaching them how to make better decisions based on the real results they want to experience. *Decide* explores what drives us to do the things we do each day. It explains that the things we don't have to do at all matter the most in defining us as leaders and as individuals. It explains how to achieve balance in our lives through better decision making, rather than waiting for an employer to provide it for us. It presents readers with a perspective on the different ways we create the energy we need to get through each day—including accomplishments and procrastination—and challenges readers to make a choice on how to get theirs. It presents an understanding of the value of time from an opportunity cost perspective and how our understanding of that value determines how we will spend our lives. It offers valuable advice on prioritizing, planning, managing interruptions, and organizing to provide real-life practical skills to apply in order to get more done in less time, reduce stress, and complete the things we have to do so we can have more time for the things that make life worth living. And last, it offers an explanation of how our decision-making habits shape our lives and relationships in the long run.

This project is the culmination of many years of content creation, idea development, live presentations, audience polling and brainstorming, research, and soul-searching on the topics of time management and personal leadership. I have spent many years in the talent development industry because I believe in its mission to help people think and reflect about their values, to take responsibility for their lives, to take a step back and recalibrate when new direction is needed, and to provide the framework within which people can evaluate their decisions, direction, and vision of the future.

I also believe in the power of this industry to help businesses form vision, missions, common culture, and meaningful purpose, as well as the road maps to fulfill them. Employee development, as part of a company's mission, has been linked to happier employees, happier customers, and longer retention of both. These metrics improve not only the general wellness of an organization but also productivity and the bottom line. After attending my leadership programs, clients have reported increased engagement, improved retention, and intensified corporate culture. Leadership is essential for companies to survive and thrive in a fast-changing world. I especially believe my definition of *leadership* as "improvement" is necessary in business and in life. Without constant improvement, organizations begin to fall behind and die out. As individuals, the same thing is true. Personal leadership, pursuing Gain and adhering to values, is what gets us out of the rut and allows us to grow and improve over time.

Leadership and progress take time, energy, and commitment. But time continues to pass, whether you use it to accomplish something worthwhile or not. If your decisions about life and how you use your time do not reflect an effort to make the future better than it is today, then it won't be. Pursuing Gain, making proactive choices, and considering the consequences of your actions or inactions on your employees, family, colleagues, friends, and children define you as a leader, because you are improving things and determining what the future can be rather than leaving it to chance.

My passion for cultivating leadership at all levels has driven me to develop this material and present it to thousands of people every year. After hearing people around the world tell stories about their leadership experiences, I can tell you that leaders really do make a difference. So I hope you decide to be a leader and to make a difference, and I hope this book will show you how.

If, after reading this book, you decide and commit to making improvements in your life and leading toward a more passionate, engaged future, then *Decide* has accomplished its purpose.

Introduction

September 16 was always a great day during my childhood. Once per year, every year, for at least 18 years, it was the only day I got to decide what I would eat for dinner. It was my birthday.

With 12 kids, a husband, and various guests in the house every evening, my mother would had to have been crazy to take orders and try to satisfy everyone. So every day, she surveyed the pantry and made the decision herself regarding what everyone in the family would be eating that night. The only time this wasn't the case was on someone's birthday. Then the royal treatment was bestowed, and everyone had to eat *your* favorite that night. I remember what each person's favorite was and the look of pride and satisfaction on each one's face when it was served. I also remember the rarely successful negotiations my siblings and I undertook in trying to influence the birthday kid's choice. Everyone understood the value of the opportunity in front of them. No one was naïve enough to let that feeling of power and freedom of choice slip by for another year.

Lucky for us, the meals, although undemocratically chosen for us, were always enjoyable—and always welcomed as something we didn't have to do for ourselves. The fact was, there was a lot you had to do for yourself from a young age in a family this big. For the record, Mom was a fair-minded person and a believer in free will, so for the 364 days of the year on which the meal choice was not up to you, an alternative meal of cereal and milk was always available. You still had to sit at the table with everyone, but your cereal bowl was the statement of individuality that would satisfy even the crankiest child among us.

Mom didn't make the choice as a reminder of who was in charge. She had constraints: time, budget, only two hands, and one kitchen. Thankfully she didn't have to deal with any food allergies, but there was no shortage of strong opinions. Almost every night there was someone who chose the cereal.

When I anticipated going away to college, I was excited about my visions of the independence I would have living in a dorm. I knew there would be many choices available to me regarding schools, majors, how to use my time once I was there, and so on. But I had to laugh the first time I went to the campus cafeteria and found that there was a limited, predetermined menu every day, and there was a large cereal dispenser at the end of the tray line in case you didn't like what they were offering.

That rush of pride and freedom that comes from the authority to make our own choices, our own decisions, is a powerful feeling to experience. Even as children, we recognized the power of having choices. Obviously, as we mature, the process of making decisions moves from what we once considered a cherished privilege to a significant responsibility. This usually happens as the consequences of those decisions become more serious and lasting. The bigger the decisions we make, the more the results begin to affect other people, like our family or employees. Sooner or later, making decisions can even feel like a burden to the point where you sometimes just want someone else to tell you what to do or pursue next and how to get there . . . or at least just to decide what's for dinner.

Although most of the decisions we make result in a good meal choice or affect similarly insignificant matters, some have a significant impact on our lives. Do these things deserve equal amounts of time and attention? How do you decide how to prioritize them? Do you know where to start when it's time to make a crucial decision?

Let me ask you some other important questions: How do you feel about the big decisions you've made so far? What about the everyday choices that affect your daily life? Does your life feel balanced? Do you have enough time to get to the important things, or are you always running in place trying to keep up? Do you know how to prioritize and plan effectively to get more done in less time? Can making better decisions produce better results? Do you know how to progress from managing to leading? Are you fully engaged in your career and your goals? Do you find ways to improve your business and your life while still managing and maintaining the daily business of just *being you*? This book will show you that these things are not only possible, but indeed *they are necessary* to prevent burnout, maintain happiness, and become an effective leader in your business and in your life.

Chapter 1 Two Forms of Human Motivation

Gain and Prevent Pain

Twenty years from now you will be more disappointed by the things you didn't do than by the ones you did do. So throw off the bowlines. Sail away from the safe harbor. Catch the trade winds in your sails. Explore. Dream. Discover.
—Mark Twain

What decisions or pursuits produce significant results in our lives—and are we giving them enough time and attention? Which of the many things that we do each day actually move us forward, and which just keep us running in place?

According to popular psychology, we all have the same reasons for doing the hundreds of tasks that we do each day. Many psychology studies have agreed that we can divide all sources of human motivation into two categories: to move toward Gain, or Prevent Pain. Every time you've felt compelled to do *anything*—from making a phone call, to getting up off the couch, to spending money, to going to work, to traveling, you were either motivated to move toward something you want (Gain), or prevent the loss of something you have (Prevent Pain).

We can illustrate this concept in almost any part of your life: health, finances, eating, career/work, even family and hobbies. Let's look at your health first. Do you exercise regularly, take vitamins or medications, or see doctors for checkups or when you feel ill? Every time you're motivated to do something about your health, it has either been to Gain in that category (get healthier than you are now, lose weight, lower cholesterol levels, tone muscles, heal injuries) or to Prevent Pain (prevent illness, weight gain, disease, muscle deterioration, and so forth). Sometimes you can have *both* motivations for doing something; for instance, you might exercise to lose weight *and* to prevent heart disease.

How about your finances? Everyone has been motivated by money at some point in his or her life. Are you trying to Gain in this category by getting a promotion and a raise, making a profitable investment, or increasing your savings? Or are you trying to Prevent Pain—that is, keep from losing the money you have—by buying insurance, clipping coupons, applying for a scholarship or grant, refinancing your mortgage, or finding a cheaper place to live?

Then, of course, there's food and eating. Sometimes you want to Gain a fine dining experience or try a new type of cuisine. Sometimes you are far too hungry or busy for that and just need to eat something to prevent hunger pains or headaches and be done with it so you can get back to work.

The Gain versus Pain question applies in business as well. Ask yourself: Is the purpose of your weekly meeting to identify new target clients or figure out how to improve the process of taking new orders? Or do you use it to go over meeting protocols and talk about employee lateness or inventory status? Is it a Gain meeting that will move your business forward, or is it a Prevent Pain meeting that will simply keep you from falling behind?

Consider any motivation you've recently had about your career. Has it been focused on Gain tasks that would benefit your career in the long term, such as pursuing an advanced degree, earning a professional certification, or closing a landmark deal that could put you in the running for a promotion? Or are you thinking more about how to avoid the next round of layoffs that may be coming or what needs to be done to meet expectations on your next performance appraisal?

Either Gain or Prevent Pain pushes you toward completing every decision and activity you pursue. And although it could be a combination of both, one is always in the majority. You have 51 percent or more of one of these motivations driving you to do that specific task. The most important difference between the two is the results they produce.

> **Tasks that you are driven toward by Gain produce more significant positive results in your life and your business than tasks that you are driven toward by Prevent Pain.**

You might immediately wonder why. When you are thinking about Gain and you are being motivated by Gain, you are focusing on something you *want*. You are figuring out how to produce a result that you *desire* in your life. You are not thinking about losing something or maintaining the status quo. You are working to move your life forward from where it is now, making it better than what it is today, considering how you *desire* your life to be—and that's exciting! Gain gives you focus, a direction to head toward.

These aren't the thoughts that cross our mind as we do our everyday Prevent Pain tasks such as paying bills and doing laundry. Clean laundry isn't something we *desire* out of life. When we do laundry we are preventing the pain of having no clean clothes to wear. Similarly, paying bills prevents the pain of having our electricity turned off or having to pay late fees to the credit card company. But focusing on a Gain is different. It pushes us to move toward something we *want*, something that will make our lives better. And those results are much more significant to our lives than the results that Prevent Pain tasks produce.

Take a minute to think of something you'd love to do or achieve in life that you haven't already done. There is no right or wrong answer; this is uniquely you. Have you always dreamed of getting an MBA or PhD, finishing a marathon, learning a new language, writing a book, opening a business, starting a foundation, or restoring a vintage car? What about learning a new sport, traveling to foreign countries, or researching your family tree? How about buying your first house, owning an income property, or running for political office? Think of one thing that stands out among all the others. What would you most love to do in life that you haven't already done?

Now, would you say that this goal or accomplishment is about moving toward something you want or preventing the loss of something you have? For most people, it's about *Gain*. Few people, when asked to identify something they would love to do in life, talk about paying their electric bill or filing an expense report. *When we think about things we want to accomplish in life, we are thinking about Gain.* Consider what your life would be like if you accomplished that Gain task. Would it bring you pride, a sense of accomplishment, and happy memories? Would your life be better than it is today?

That's what Gain is about: improving life and moving forward. It's about the experiences and accomplishments that you *want* to have as a part of your life.

PREVENT PAIN: I HAVE TO DO IT!

Prevent Pain tasks simply prompt us to do what we have to do. There's that old saying that the only certainties in life are death and taxes. However, I'm sure that if I asked you what you have to do today (or any day) in order to keep up, you would have a much longer list.

Everyone has responsibilities; some more than others based on our age, job, family, and so forth. There are many "have to" responsibilities that simply come with earning a paycheck; after all, your employer is paying you to take care of certain tasks. If you are in school, you have to study and take advantage of the opportunity to learn and prepare for your future. Things such as home ownership, car ownership, and even pet ownership come with big responsibilities. Parenting is in a category by itself when it comes to taking on responsibilities and all the "have to" tasks that come with it. Some responsibilities, such as dealing with illness or injury, may have come to you without your consent; some you may have willingly signed up for; others may have come as an indirect result of your decisions.

No matter how many "have to" tasks are on your plate, you can always fill your day with them. There's always something to repair, maintain, clean, feed, keep up with, pay for, or care for. The reason that Prevent Pain tasks go on and on is that they never actually go away; they just eventually repeat. For example, you don't really cross doing dishes off your to-do list; you just move it to the bottom because by the next night, you will have to wash them again. The same is true with checking e-mail or stocking inventory. You don't cross it off; you move it down the list, because it's coming back again at some point. Tasks such as putting gas in your car, doing laundry, and going grocery shopping all have to be done over and over again because the things necessary to maintain your life are never finished. By always focusing on getting them done and preventing pain, you don't end up with Gain; you end up with no pain and unfortunately no progress.

Prevent Pain tasks come with varying degrees of urgency. You have to complete some, such as a certain assignment for work, according to deadlines. Others, such as housecleaning, have a bit more flexibility in terms of timeline; it's your responsibility to get them done sometime or deal with the consequences of failing to complete them. There is one thing that all "have to" tasks have in common, which is our definition of a *have to*: a "have to" (or Prevent Pain task) is any task or activity that, if neglected, someone else will eventually bring to your attention.

For instance, let's say someone is waiting for you to complete a task. If you don't do it, the person waiting will eventually catch you at the elevator, call you on the phone, send you an e-mail, stop you in the hall, send a reminder in the mail, or come knocking on your door and say, "Hey, did you ever get a chance to . . . ?" Whether it's a manager, colleague, client, family member, neighbor, roommate, bill collector, or someone else, that person will want to know if you did what you were supposed to do. That is the nature of a "have to," or Prevent Pain, task. The pain that you should have prevented will visit you eventually if you don't complete it.

DO I REALLY HAVE TO?

When I say "have to," you may think, "I don't *have to* do anything; I am a free person!" And sure, the decision about whether or not to complete these tasks *is* technically up to you. However, if you decide *not* to do them, you will have to face the consequences of that decision. For example, if you decide you will stop paying your rent or mortgage, you will have to deal with the consequences of not being able to live in your home anymore and possibly not being able to get another one because of your destroyed credit. So you either have to pay it, or you have to deal with what happens if you don't. The consequences are the pain you are preventing when you complete a Prevent Pain task.

Although I doubt anyone wants to risk becoming homeless, some unfinished Prevent Pain tasks have less severe consequences that you may choose to accept instead of doing the task. For example, if your neighbor knocks on your door and says, "Hey, did your yard become the Amazon? When are you going to mow it?" you could respond in any number of ways, including, "Hey, thanks for bringing that to my attention, *but I'm not doing it ever again!* It's my yard, and I can do what I please with it!" You have made your decision to stop mowing the lawn, to not complete this Prevent Pain task. But now the pain that wasn't prevented will start to roll in: your yard looks overgrown, and you can't use it for anything; your grass might die; and your relationship with your neighbors will suffer. If you let it go long enough, your kids or pets might even get lost out there! If you can live with these consequences, then you might choose this course of action, but either way, mowing the lawn is a "have to" or Prevent Pain because you either have to do it or you have to deal with the consequences of not doing it.

This is how you can distinguish between Gain and Prevent Pain tasks. There is no "have to" with a Gain task, because there are no consequences if you choose not to pursue Gain in your life.

And yet it is the Gain tasks, the things that you *never* have to do, that will produce the most significant positive results in your life and in your business. It seems a little backward, doesn't it? You would think that if something is required, then you should be congratulated for getting it done. But that's not how it works. If you continue to do solely what is necessary to survive every day, all you will accomplish is preventing pain from coming your way. To move your life or your business forward from where it is today and to see an improvement, you must do something extraordinary—something that you didn't have to do at all. You must pursue Gain.

This concept first came to me when I was about to graduate from college. I did well in school, but I didn't have the highest grades in my graduating class. In addition to studying, taking tests, and writing research papers, I played football and volunteered a lot of my time with various groups. In particular, I had been a Big Brother to a great kid from the city since my freshman year. I always liked and was grateful for the fact that I had choices. Therefore, I thought a great way to spend my extra time would be to offer some positive choices to a kid who wouldn't otherwise have any. I spent a lot of time with him playing sports, going to movies, and helping him with his homework, among other things.

As graduation approached and I was scrambling to complete papers and exams like everyone else, I received a surprising call from the Graduation Committee. They chose me as the Valedictorian Speaker for the graduation ceremony. The committee, which was composed of faculty, advisors, and students, didn't choose me because of exam scores and academic prowess. They informed me that I had been chosen because of all the extra things I did while I was in college that I *didn't have to do*, like being in the Big Brother program, serving on student government, and hosting my own campus radio show. None of the activities they mentioned was required for graduation.

At the time, that struck me as strange. Some students in my class had higher grades than I did and were doing a better job at what was *required* to graduate, but they were not chosen for this high honor. Instead the committee chose me because of all the things I did that I *didn't* have to do at all! The more time I spent thinking about this, the more I began to understand. Everyone had to pass their classes to graduate, and many students had high grades; but that wasn't enough to differentiate them from everyone else. It was the Gain I pursued that separated me from my peers. The decisions I made regarding how to spend my time and energy is what built my identity. When those people on the committee thought of me, they weren't asking, "Is he keeping up with what he has to do?"; they were asking, "What is different about him? What choices did he make? What did he do that he didn't have to do?"

This experience and this way of differentiating myself always stayed with me. It provided evidence of the power and the significant positive results that can come when we decide to do more than just what we have to do. These results can come only from Gain.

ATTRIBUTES OF A GAIN TASK

If we examine the attributes of a Gain task, we can discern exactly which tasks we can label as Gain and which we can label Prevent Pain. It will also help you figure out how you feel when you are doing each. (Hint: You'll soon see why one makes you feel *accomplished* while the other just makes you feel *busy*.) Once we identify these attributes, we can look at the results that are achieved from spending time doing each kind of task. We can then consider whether this difference in results should influence the decisions you make regarding how to spend your time.

1. A Gain Task Is *Never Urgent*

Urgency is a great human motivator. Just *labeling* something as urgent makes people sit up and stress over what they may have missed and what is due right away. But when it comes to results, urgency alone can't deliver. It is not a great criterion for deciding what is most important or what will produce the most significant results in your life.

For example, you've already identified something that you would love to do in life that you haven't already done. Think about that particular Gain task. Is it necessary for you to get started on it *today*? What if you are really busy this week; can it wait until next week, or even next month? What if you went an entire year without doing anything about that Gain task? Would anything bad happen? No. A Gain task can *always wait*; there are no deadlines or reports due for it. You don't owe it to anyone. There are no consequences for not doing it. Your only motivation to do it is to improve your life in some way. It is never an urgent situation. Therefore, if you base your decisions regarding what to do with your time solely on what is urgent, you won't be doing any Gain tasks—and you won't experience the significant positive results that come from Gain.

In contrast, you can't delay or ignore Prevent Pain tasks. For instance, how long can you go without food? People have made it 30 to 45 days in extreme circumstances without food. People have lived two to three days without water in extreme cases. The urgency of finding food and water, paying your mortgage, turning in a proposal on time, and showing up for work is obvious. These things have deadlines and consequences if you don't do them.

2. You Don't Have to Complete a Gain Task

The second attribute for a Gain task is *you don't have to do it*. Motivation to complete a Gain task comes from the opportunity to gain improvement and results in your life, not from fear of the consequences that may arise if you *don't* do it. No one will ever ask you about it or follow up on it. There's only one reason why you would do it: because you *want* to, not because you *have* to.

What happens if you *never* complete any Gain tasks? Well, nothing, really. If you never do anything about a goal, no one will ever impose a fine or penalty on you; no one will ever ask why you didn't do it. Nothing bad will happen, but *nothing great will happen either*. You will not experience that Gain in your life. You won't move toward that goal or enjoy improvement. Your life will stay the same for as long as you let it.

You can go through a lifetime without ever doing anything about your Gain task. People have lived a long, happy, full lifetime without ever accomplishing that particular goal. The reason to complete this goal is because you desire the results that task would bring. The difference between the Gain and the Prevent Pain tasks is the difference between *I want to* and *I have to*, the difference between *don't have to* and *have to*, and the difference between motivation stemming from the desire for results and motivation driven by the fear of consequences.

If you achieved the Gain task that you identified, would it produce significant or insignificant results? Don't think of *results* solely in terms of how much money you will make from it, how it will look on a résumé, or what other people will think. Think about how accomplishing or experiencing the Gain task makes you feel, and how it will enhance your life; in that way, think of the results as the memories, feelings, progress, growth, and improvement in your life.

Completing a Gain task should produce *significant* results; otherwise, you wouldn't do it. If you are choosing to spend your time on something that you don't have to do but that you really *want* to do, you are working to enhance your life. Whether it's volunteering, developing a new skill, improving a process at work, or engaging in anything else that we "don't have to" do, *whenever we are motivated by Gain, we are thinking about the results our time and effort will bring us*—in our lives, in our relationships, and in our business.

3. You Can't Delegate a Gain Task to Anyone Else

The nature of a Gain goal or accomplishment means that *only you* can achieve the results you seek. And *only you* can experience the satisfaction and improvement that comes from them. You can't delegate your goals and dreams to another person.

We are all faced with the question of how to best spend our allotted 24 hours every day to get the most out of them. Every time you take on a task, you make a decision to spend the amount of time that the task will take. *And every time you do something that someone else could do for you, you are giving up the opportunity to pursue Gain.* Everything you hire or ask another person to do—from having your shirts dry-cleaned to hiring a lawn service to maintain your yard to ordering pizza for dinner— is delegation. Even when you buy clothes at a retail store, instead of making them yourself, you are delegating! Almost every time you spend money, you are delegating someone else to do something for you.

The question is, are you delegating *enough?* If you're spending time completing Prevent Pain tasks that someone else could complete, you're missing out on chances to advance your business, relationships, or life. You are giving up the opportunity to pursue Gain when you don't delegate effectively.

Of course, there is much to consider when you decide to delegate. Is there someone who is more *available* than you are? Do *time and urgency* matter? Is someone else *more talented or more skilled* at a given task? Does *quality* matter? If it's a professional task: Does someone else need to complete it for education or succession planning, to grow, learn, or develop part of their job? How much will it cost your organization for you versus someone else to complete it? But the number one question to consider is, *What else could you be doing with your time if you weren't doing that task?* Most likely the answer would have something to do with pursuing Gain in some area of your life.

The result of a Gain task is achieving a sense of *leadership* in your life, your business, or your relationships—and finding time for leadership is difficult without delegation. Have you ever wondered where you might find the time to think outside the box, to work *on* the systems as opposed to working *in* the systems, to *improve* the business rather than to *do* daily business, to develop strategies rather than to spin wheels and waste time doing things the old way?

> *Delegation* is where the time comes from for us to move things forward.

What should you delegate that would give you more time to improve your expertise in a certain area? If you had more time, what could you reach expert status doing? If you reached this expert status, what new solutions could you come up with for your employer or your clients? The more valuable those solutions are, the more valuable you become.

Delegation is a necessary tool because limited time is the number one obstacle to learning, growing, and pursuing goals. It is the key strategic skill that enables you to spend time moving your life forward versus staying where you are.

I learned this lesson several years ago when my business was taking off. The phone was ringing every day with presentation opportunities. It was a sign of a good economy, as well as the good reputation I had built with a few years of satisfied customers with word-of-mouth power. And it felt great! I had been pounding the pavement (so to speak), cold-calling clients for the first few years, and my efforts were finally paying off. In fact, I was getting so busy that I would respond to a voice mail asking about presentation dates with a quick e-mail to confirm, hoping everything went well. I had no time for in-depth contract discussions or long sales calls.

I was speaking or training four to five times per week, which meant customizing material, preparing handouts, and making travel arrangements at night or on the weekends. Although I was excited about the business, the hours were killing me—and I knew I needed help. The problem, of course, was carving out the time to find the right people to help me. I was scared to death that I'd hire the wrong people and have employee issues on top of everything else. Months went by with little sleep and lots of stress. Not only did I need to delegate some of my responsibilities to someone, but I also needed to delegate the task of finding the right person because I didn't have time to do it!

I finally reached my breaking point; then I came up with a simple plan and ran with it. It started with babysitters. My wife, who has an MBA in finance, was up to her eyeballs in daily work having to do with four small kids at home. So the first step was to make a quick call to my sister, who works at a local high school. She sent over several eager young students to our house every day after school to provide our children with supervision and fun from 3:00 to 5:00 PM (for no more than $10 per hour). This gave my wife two hours every day to do what I had no time to do: find our first employee. She attacked career websites for several weeks and came up with 400 résumés. She then researched these people on social media, looking for someone with the right profile for our business, the right personality fit for us, and the right skills to help us out. She weaned the crop down to about 15 people and presented them to me.

I chose four résumés that looked like they were just what I needed. We interviewed each person—and I hired one! We got our new executive assistant quickly up to speed on what we do and needed *her* to do. Within a few days, she was making travel arrangements for me and took over invoicing and website management.

My wife then started using the babysitter time to work on our business every day. I went from being a one-man show to having an executive assistant and a part-time MBA consultant in the course of a few weeks. We contracted with several more professionals along the way, and I began to feel like a person again.

Just a few months earlier, my business had hit an unsustainable growth point. With the right delegation, we moved beyond it, made it sustainable, and thrived. With the management of Prevent Pain tasks such as travel arrangements, billing, and advertising taken off my plate, I was free to actually think about where I wanted to go next with my business and spend more time in the Gain category.

Managing my business was taking all of my time, but my business was ready for *leadership*. Delegating gave me the time to provide that leadership and move my business forward.

MANAGEMENT VERSUS LEADERSHIP

What's the difference between management and leadership—and what does it have to do with Gain and Prevent Pain and managing your decisions?

As we've seen, Prevent Pain tasks keep your life or business *the way they are today*. Paying your mortgage, doing your laundry, showing up for work on time, and handing in your reports on time are all about maintaining the status quo and keeping your life in the state it's currently in.

If you complete these and all other Prevent Pain tasks, you're doing a great job of *managing* your job and life without facing any consequences or falling behind on your responsibilities. Management is *maintenance*—keeping things the way they are today. If all you do is maintain for the next five years, what will your career and life look like half a decade from now? Pretty much the same as it does today. And perhaps that's not a bad thing for you. I'm not discounting the effectiveness of management. Having a well-managed life, business, or relationship is something to be proud of. Good management is vital to your success in business and in life, but *it is not leadership*. If you want things to be better than they are today, you need leadership.

If management is maintenance, then leadership is *improvement*—moving things forward from where they are today and making them better. What will be different and better in your life five years from now? The answer to that question lies in whatever Gain tasks you decide to take on.

Management is keeping things the way they are today.

Management = Maintenance

Leadership is moving things forward from where they are today.

Leadership = Improvement

Are you deliberately determining where your life is going? Or are you just managing it and making sure you keep up with the minimum requirements of what you have to do each day to Prevent Pain?

We should be asking that question in business much more often than we are. I have met many people in business over the years who were supposed to be in leadership roles but who actually made things worse! They ran divisions out of profitability, drove companies out of business, cost their organizations millions of dollars, and lost some of their largest customers. That's not leadership; it's *mis*management, which leads to decay and deterioration. True leadership does not depend on a title or a position. Having a position of authority in a group *gives you the opportunity* to make decisions that improve or change things. But if things *don't* get better as a result, then you are not a leader.

This turns leadership from a somewhat fuzzy concept into a *result* that you must produce. If you have made good decisions, identified Gain tasks, and are moving toward those goals, then you are truly *leading yourself* toward a better life. If you have grown and developed your business, then you have proved your *leadership*, regardless of your title or position. True leadership doesn't require a title. If you want to be a leader, all you have to do is *make things better*. And every member of a group can tell who is making things better, who is making things worse, and who is doing a great job of maintaining or managing things. Anyone who is improving things is a leader. Changes in economies, technologies, trends, cycles, and employee landscapes require changes in thinking and improving the way things are done. Leaders have the guts to put forth changes and new ideas for the future of the organization.

This definition of leadership means that *anyone* in an organization can be a leader as long as he or she is focused on the betterment of the organization. But it also raises the question:

Who in *your life* can be a leader except *you*?

Doing what we have to do each day to maintain our lives is *management*. This is not what defines us as individuals; rather, it is what makes us *the same* as everyone else. *Personal leadership* is doing what we don't have to do to lead ourselves forward and grow each day. This is where we get our self-identity, and what differentiates us from others. If we don't get our identity from Gain tasks, then we're left to determine it based on how we compare to other people. And this is a breeding ground for negativity, mistrust, jealousy, and depression, as well superiority or inferiority thinking. We must continuously adapt, grow, and improve to lead ourselves forward as things around us change—and to avoid getting stuck in a rut. The way to do that is through personal leadership, or Gain, which we will talk more about in the next chapter.

THE ONE AND ONLY EXERCISE I WILL ASK YOU TO DO IN THIS BOOK . . . BRAINSTORM!

Before we move on, I want you to think a little more about Gain for a few minutes. What are the Gain tasks or pursuits that would move your life forward? What would make your life better? Throughout this book, we will be exploring how your decisions about how you spend your time result in the quality of life that you experience—and how that experience could be better if you insert more Gain into your life. We will also explore how to better manage all your daily tasks while improving your life at the same time.

To prepare for that, take 5 or 10 minutes and brainstorm a list of Gain pursuits that, if accomplished, would make your life better than it is today, regardless of how long it would take to accomplish them—and *write them down*. Consider both long- and short-term professional and personal goals. Think about your career, family life, relationships, home, health, travels, hobbies, interests, finances, community, circle of friends, neighborhood, and on and on. You want these to be things that you would love to do or experience in life that you haven't already. The more you can imagine, the better.

Remember, thinking about all the ways that your life could improve doesn't mean you are dissatisfied with where you are now. It just means that you're considering ways to improve and move, what you want for your life, and what would make things better. Spend a few minutes thinking about what your life would be like if you accomplished one or two or *all* of those improvements.

Your goals, or Gain tasks, may be as diverse as going to law school, climbing a mountain, getting a promotion, planting a garden, opening your own business, learning a new language, adopting a child, and painting copies of famous Impressionist art. Whatever you put on it, *keep your list*. You may want to refer or add to it as you make your way through this book and envision what Gain can do for you.

Chapter 2 It's All up to You
Avoid Burnout and Create Balance

To me, if life boils down to one thing, it's movement. To live is to keep moving.

—Jerry Seinfeld

It should be clear by now which of your tasks are Gain and which are Prevent Pain. However, it might also have become clear that you are so busy with all of your Prevent Pain tasks that it would feel like Gain if you could just accomplish everything on your to-do list! I hear this all the time during my presentations. People say things like:

> "How on Earth can I take on Gain and try to do more? I'm no overachiever!"

> "I'd be happy if I could just get to the work that I have to do!"

> "I have more to do at work and at home than I have time for already!"

> "My list of goals is buried under a pile of stuff I have to do!"

SO WHY TAKE ON GAIN?

It's true that taking on Gain while you are buried in Prevent Pain can seem rather impossible or sadistic. Most people, after a long day at work, try to spend some time with family while facing the ever-present question of what to make for dinner before tackling chores, doing housework, and paying bills. After all of that, it's hard to imagine being able to muster up the energy to do anything more intelligent than watch a sitcom on TV before heading to bed to get those precious 7 hours of rest . . . just to do it all over again the next day. Pursuing your long-term goals is the furthest thing from your mind when you are at a point of exhaustion and frustration with daily life. It is too difficult to think about pursuing Gain if we wait until all our energy is spent on Preventing Pain. However, if all you *ever* do is Prevent Pain, you'll eventually start to feel like you are out of balance, which leads to *burnout*.

Burning out like this is a serious and potentially very expensive problem, especially when you consider that it can affect the health of some people, necessitating the purchase of antidepressants and anxiety medications, or be the cause of a classic midlife crisis in others, resulting in thrill-seeking purchases such as skydiving lessons, a new sports car, or a motorcycle. Burnout causes painful psychological and physiological consequences. People feel this way when they've been in a rut for too long, doing the same thing day after day, not making any progress. *A rut is the absence of life getting better.* When people feel that they have been working too hard for too long and have nothing to show for it, they experience burnout. In fact, not only are their lives *not getting better*, but their negative outlook causes their personal relationships to suffer. Their health begins to deteriorate because of their physical manifestations of stress. Their wealth takes a blow, because they make impulse purchases to satisfy their need for excitement or work fewer hours, having no motivation or ambition to work.

So how do you avoid burnout with everything you have to do, manage, and maintain? How do you find balance? *The answer is to insert Gain into your life.* Pursuing Gain tasks and obtaining the results they produce are what keep you from feeling like you are spinning your wheels and not pleasing anyone (including yourself). It prevents you from working hard but failing to create anything of significance. Identifying a Gain task that would produce significant results toward the life you want or progress toward a goal you have makes all your work *worth the effort.* Gain tasks help you feel balanced because of the positive results they produce in your life—results that *you* identified as something *you* want. When you are achieving something you want, you feel balanced.

You might be wondering, "How does *working even harder* toward pursuing Gain keep you feeling *balanced?* How can *adding* responsibilities *reduce* your level of stress?"

THE PARADOX OF BALANCE

A 2010 survey conducted by one think tank found that 90 percent of working mothers and 95 percent of working fathers reported experiencing work-family conflict. A different survey in 2012 produced similar results: 88 percent of employees claimed that they have a hard time juggling work and life. Fifty-seven percent cited it as a "significant problem" in their lives, while 64 percent claimed to be "physically exhausted" when they get home from work. How can the numbers be that high? And how long can that kind of stress be sustainable in the employee landscape?

I recently held a consulting session with one of my clients regarding the issues her company was facing. She asked me to stay away from the topic of work-life balance because, in her opinion, "There is no such thing." This company was dealing with the consequences of stress and burnout in the workplace: poor morale, disengagement, reduced productivity, retention problems, absenteeism, higher health care costs, on-the-job errors, lower-quality work product, and poor customer experience ratings. Employers recognize that stressed, out-of-balance, or burned out employees affect all these things, which ultimately affect not only personal wellness but the organization's bottom line. The stakes are high. So why has work-life balance been so hard to figure out?

The problem is that employers can't provide balance as part of a benefits package. Regardless of their best efforts or claims, one organization can't offer more of it to its employees than another. If it could, everyone would want to work there. (See Figure 2.1.)

Although many companies do their best by offering perks such as a flexible work schedule, child care, or financial services, these things can only help you *manage* life more efficiently. They can't give your life direction, momentum, or balance.

FIGURE 2.1

Despite recognizing the problem, survey after survey shows that employees have been driven further away from achieving work-life balance over the past decade. Common messages include "record high unemployment," "if we can survive this economy," and "doing more with less." Each of us has been forced to value the fact that we simply *have* a job, regardless of how much stress we are under. Many people have had to take on more responsibility and more tasks just to *stay where they are* in their careers. Each day has become a race to complete our to-do list and meet expectations. But that is not seeking balance; that is seeking survival. And remaining in survival mode for too long without making progress eventually leads to burnout.

The idea of work-life balance is inherently combative. It suggests a discord between two vital parts of life: work being what we *have to* do, and life being what we *want to* do. It suggests that these are two opposing forces between which we must constantly make choices—and that when we choose to give time or thought to one, the other loses. This constant battle between work and personal pursuits puts one in a perpetual state of conflict; furthermore, it suggests that personal and professional goals are out of alignment or mutually exclusive and that achieving both is therefore unattainable.

It sounds like people believe there is an inherent conflict between work and life! This is an unfortunate perspective, because you *don't* have a separate professional life and personal life; you have only a life. This dichotomy leads people to say things like they want to work really hard and retire at 50 and have the "rest of their lives to do what they want." But does that produce balance? Would it be wise to wait until your life is half over before you start living it? Would your spouse or friends even wait around that long to enjoy it with you?

Trying to manage the clock on a daily basis doesn't guarantee balance either. Spending half of each day in the office and half at home can't guarantee that you would leave stress behind when you left work for the day. It won't ensure satisfying personal relationships because you spend a certain number of hours outside the office or because you turn your phone off during dinner. There is no quantitative measure for balance.

The number of hours that people spend at work per week is not a good indicator of how balanced people feel. Often, people in extreme jobs— those who work 60 to 100 hours per week in high-paying professional positions—report that they love what they do and thrive on the pressure. They pursue Gain every day in their jobs. Because they work to the extreme, they also report extreme escapes when necessary. Some of them take vacations to remote locations, such as the far northern reaches of Canada, where there are no cell phone signals or Internet connections, trying to completely disconnect themselves from the office to ensure there isn't any possibility of mobile communication. They engage in extreme sports or adventures to forget about the pressures of work. It sounds to me like they are working until they're half dead during the week and then risking finishing themselves off on the weekends, but these people do *nothing but pursue Gain*! They survive their grueling hours and demands by being in constant pursuit of goals that, for them, are moving the company forward each day and pushing their physical limits in their spare time. Of course, not all those who work this hard report being this committed. Many young executives quit by the five-year mark to pursue less demanding roles, citing the brutal hours and demands of extreme working as hazardous to their health and family life. In Japan, death by overwork has happened so often that there is actually a word for it: *karoshi*.

Conversely, some people who work much more normal hours can report all the stress and depression associated with burnout and overwork syndromes. There are countless articles targeted at stressed-out women and out-of-balance men, suggesting cure-all answers such as drinking more water, eating a healthy diet, and seeking more sunlight to create work-life balance. Although doing these things can improve your health and lower stress, they cannot cure the feeling that your life's rewards are not worth its efforts.

GAIN IS THE ANSWER TO THE BALANCE CRISIS

The only one who can create balance in your life is you. And the only way to create it is to seek to make your life better today than it was yesterday. You do that by pursuing Gain. Think of the last time you felt as though your life was better today than it was yesterday. Maybe it was graduating, getting a new job offer, receiving a promotion, landing a new client, receiving an award, taking a great vacation, running a marathon, hosting a great event, starting a new relationship, embarking on a new volunteer opportunity, helping a child with a new milestone, solving an old problem with a fresh new thought, or even just getting a great workout or receiving a compliment on a job well done. These are times when you felt *balanced*. You worked toward a goal, and your hard work produced real results and made an improvement in your (and probably, someone else's) life. That's what goals do for us. They make our lives better today than they were yesterday.

Moving toward our goals *creates balance* and the excitement that we need to keep going. It offers a sense of assurance that we have not wasted our time, have identified where we want to go, and have done something about it instead of just standing still and aging through another day. The momentum and results that improvement creates inspire us to do even more the next day.

> *Balance* is a feeling you get when you are satisfied with where you are and where you are going in life.

This is a different understanding of balance. It comes when you are satisfied with where you're spending your time and resources. It's the balance of "have to" and "don't have to," of maintenance and improvement, of management and leadership. It comes from pursuing and achieving goals and seeing improvement in your life, rather than continuing to put forth all of your effort toward maintenance or standing still. As you take your life from where it was stuck and move it toward a goal, you get excited about the improvement. You achieve peace of mind when you know that you have finally done something about what you are claiming is important to you.

The balance and satisfaction that come from pursuing goals and improvement is unique to each individual. What makes one person's life better might not be what someone else wants. One person might want to buy a bigger house, while another is looking to finally downsize. It's not always bigger, better, more; it's about *movement*, taking your life in the direction you want it to go and experiencing the excitement and exhilaration that goes with it. When someone says to you, "I have a goal," that person is really saying, "Achieving this would make my life better."

There is always opportunity for improvement, ingenuity, new adventure, and new growth, both personally and professionally. The best way to combat burnout and stress—and achieve a feeling that your life is balanced between what you have to do and what makes you feel alive—is to *continuously seek improvement in some area of your life.*

This is important, because life's responsibilities and worries never stop. In fact, they seem to grow as we get older. Consider all the parts of life that seem to get *worse* over time. If something is in a natural process of deterioration and you don't actively maintain it to keep it alive and well, it will eventually die.

The reality of aging is that health becomes more of a challenge all the time. Scientifically speaking, you will age and decline a bit every year of your life. Studies show an exponential increase in time and money spent on health care after age 50. If you don't actively exercise and maintain your physical and mental health, then you will spend every year of your life in worse health than the last.

Keeping up our physical appearance becomes more time consuming as well. Americans spend an average of $33 billion on age-related beauty products every year, and cosmetic surgery grosses $10 billion annually.[1] Dementia and other age-related mental issues are associated with 22 percent of hospitalizations and $11 billion in Medicare costs annually.[2] You can slow down the aging process and maintain and even improve your appearance or your health by working at it, but you cannot escape it entirely.

And of course, it's not just your health. Unless you move into new construction homes each year, your home will age every year as well, which means it will also require maintenance and repairs as it ages. Natural disasters such as hurricanes, floods, droughts, tornadoes, earthquakes, and so on, will cause damage and necessitate repairs, rebuilding, or relocation. No one needs a history book to recount the various economic or natural disasters that have caused many people to face these challenges year after year.

As we age, relationships can become more challenging as well, and they can take more effort to maintain as people change locations, become busy, and get tied up in the responsibilities of life.

This is especially true for businesses or careers. What if you didn't move any part of your professional life forward? If you allow your skills to remain static over time—while your competitors move forward and develop new methods of service, take advantage of new technologies, open new markets, and so on—then you will lose your clients to them as your business or career decays and eventually dies. It isn't really an option to just stay the same over time; you must improve and keep up, or become irrelevant and die out.

The truth is that lots of things deteriorate naturally throughout our lives. Problems in even *one* of these areas can put you in a rut. Thinking about all of these things at once is simply too much to bear!

Without continuous effort toward goals and progress, you will spend a great deal of time and tremendous effort on maintenance and just trying to stay where you are without losing ground. *Unless we are constantly working toward improving some area of life, we will be focused on the parts of life that naturally get worse over time.* This can cause stress, burnout, resentment, regret, and depression—not clinical depression but the despairing feeling that yesterday was better than today. We have all had that feeling at one time or another. It comes as the result of being in a rut, from experiencing these tolls that life can take without any exhilaration from accomplishment along the way. It comes from feeling that our efforts are outweighing our rewards.

Can we truly be happy if we don't have hope that the future will be better than today? Your life doesn't have to be *awful* in order to hope for a better future. You could have a great and happy life with fulfilling work, family, or friends and a satisfying level of wealth or influence. But if you always have the thought that this is *it*, this is the best it will ever be, tomorrow will be worse and the day after that will be worse and so on— you'll be miserable! I certainly don't see how you could be happy today if that was your vision of the future.

Is happiness just an issue of personal wellness, or does it also affect business's bottom line? Statistics show that depression costs employers $44 billion every year in lost productivity, which makes it among the most expensive illnesses that companies face. Conversely, happier employees were associated with higher levels of profit, productivity, retention, and customer satisfaction.[3] This is precisely why creating balance, satisfaction, and happiness has a long-term positive impact not only on you as an individual but on your organization as well.

But how do you get there? You can't just work harder to get yourself out of this type of rut. You must change direction and work toward something different.

Goals are the ticket out of any sense of depression. They improve and offset the losses or decay in our lives so we don't end up in a rut. They alleviate that feeling that you have worked hard and accomplished nothing. When you are working toward Gain, you end the day feeling like you have made progress and are moving forward. And the momentum you've created makes you feel balanced and energized—like today is *better* than yesterday, like *you* are better than you were yesterday. It gives hope for the future. It lets us sleep at night knowing that because we are working hard, things are getting better all the time. *That sounds like balance. That* sounds like satisfaction and happiness to me.

GAIN AND PREVENT PAIN MUST WORK TOGETHER

The feeling of balance comes when you have done what you had to do to maintain life and Prevent Pain *plus* you have done something you didn't have to do to move life forward a little today. So many people are in search of balance, but you can't just find balance; you have to create it by ensuring that you are seeking results that will justify your efforts. Putting forth great effort just to maintain life and keep it where it is will eventually cause burnout. However, if your efforts are focused on *producing significant results* and *moving toward improvement* every day, then the same amount of effort is justified and worthwhile.

We are constantly trying to balance goals and *improvement* with *maintenance*—the "don't have to" versus the "have to." And because these goals are different and unique to each person, no organization or employer can ever offer work-life balance. No one can achieve it for you. More time off, benefits, bonuses, and flexibility will not provide you with a sense of balance unless you use these advantages to improve your life.

Identifying Gain or goals and working toward them each day alleviates that feeling of burnout. With each small step, you see improvement and build momentum. You are moving, progressing, and the purpose of your efforts becomes more evident. You have something to talk about and develop ideas around. You find your thoughts always gravitating toward how to reach the goal and how your life will improve once you have accomplished it. You are using your resources for improvement instead of fighting to stand still. *That feeling of life in motion is creating balance.* Moving toward something meaningful that will improve life for you, your team at work, your organization, your family, and so on, is what makes depression, burnout, and stress fade away and allows balance and satisfaction to take over.

In fact, studies have reported that the most important motivator that employees felt was not the promise of raises and promotions, but rather the feeling of making progress toward a meaningful goal every day. This feeling correlated to more creativity and better-quality work. Without this feeling of progress and accomplishment, people lose the motivation to continue doing constructive work and burnout begins to set in.[4]

Even small steps can keep you balanced and improve the quality of your life overall, not just your work. We don't need to balance work and life; work is part of life. We need to balance surviving today with progressing toward a better tomorrow. If you can identify ways in which you are improving an area of your life all the time—no matter how small—then you have a credible claim to balance. The key to getting started on this journey of improvement and achieving balance in your life is to identify the opportunities for Gain in your life, then prioritize and plan.

Chapter 3 Prioritizing Tasks in Relation to Results

You rarely have time for everything you want in this life, so you need to make choices. And hopefully your choices can come from a deep sense of who you are.

—Fred Rogers

At what point in your morning routine do you first ask yourself, "What do I have to do today?" When you have listed so many things that you couldn't possibly complete them all in one day, do you then further break down the list by asking, "What is *urgent* today?" Most people prioritize their daily undertakings by asking one question: "When is it due?" The closer the deadline, the higher priority a task receives. This is a common method that prioritizes everything in relation to urgency.

If you've encountered the prioritizing models used in typical time management approaches, then you know that the letters A, B, and C have traditionally represented the urgency or the deadline that a task has. A task that's due *immediately or today* is assigned an A. Tasks that are due *soon* get a B, and a C is due next week or maybe next month, something you eventually have to complete. So really, all you need to do to turn a C into an A using this approach is to procrastinate long enough. Don't do it *now*; just wait. It will become an A at some point. Hang in there. It's coming! It seems unimportant now, and no one is asking you about it yet, but it *will* become urgent if you wait until it is due—or even overdue!

This method of prioritizing makes a task's life cycle look something like this:

> That's due in a month? Oh, that is *so* a C. I've got 30 days. I won't forget; it's important, but I have a whole month, so I'm not looking at that now . . .
>
> That's due next week, isn't it? Okay, let's make that a B. I'll put that on my radar screen. I can't let that fall through the cracks; it's coming up next week. That's huge. Okay, that's a B, but I have other things, I have As to work on today, so that will have to wait . . .
>
> That's due today?! What happened? Okay, that is my biggest A today! I need to drop everything else to get it done—this is a four-alarm fire! I need to finish this right now!

Everything you do could become an A in this approach. And when everything in life is an A, how do you know what is truly important and what isn't? This is how people live when they cancel things at the last minute. They don't show up for an event because they have a suddenly urgent matter elsewhere. They miss things that should be important to them because of things that should be *unimportant*. They have become desensitized to what means anything to them, are constantly stressed, and are under pressure to get things done—and as a result, they feel like they please no one. They are frequently late for events or places they have to be because they are always chasing some prior deadline. They feel stress over mundane things that pile up. Do you know people who live this way? Are *you* someone who lives this way?

I tell a hypothetical, animated story about taking out the trash during one of my presentations. Let's say you have a Monday morning trash pickup in your neighborhood. On Sunday night, when you are very comfortable, relaxing at home with your family, is getting up to take out the trash an A, B, or C? For most people it's a C. If you forget to do it before you go to bed, then it becomes a B on Monday morning. You still have a few hours before they come! What about when you hear the trash truck coming down the street? It's A time now, baby! Urgency has forced you to run to the street, yelling after the truck with the trash collectors cheering you on to throw your bag into the back before the truck turns the corner. You made it! Woo-hoo! What an accomplishment. Didn't it feel great? Congratulations, you have just taken out the trash. And according to that task's deadline, you have just checked off an A on your list for today. You should feel good all day about that one. However, what did you really accomplish? Not much; you really only took out the trash. And guess what? The bag inside is already filling up for next week.

This is why prioritizing in relation to urgency doesn't work. As you undoubtedly noticed, the closer we got to the deadline in this situation, the higher priority we gave the task. The task *itself* never changed, but we made it increasingly crucial as the deadline approached. This method of prioritizing gives you the illusion that you've been productive, when in reality, you have not really generated any results *that matter*. It can give you a false sense of accomplishment, a high that adds no value to your life. This is called *drama*. Drama occurs when you give something more time and attention than it deserves based on the results that it produces. Drama is *misprioritizing*.

Remember the first attribute of a Gain task: they are never urgent! The things that will bring you the greatest results in your life don't have a deadline.

A NEW WAY TO PRIORITIZE

Effective prioritizing is not based on deadlines or urgency. It is based on *results*. Effective prioritizing assigns value and order to events in advance of their occurrence and requires that you ask some new questions: What results does this task produce in your life? Which activities in your life produce the greatest results?

So here is a new way to prioritize. A, B, and C should represent *the results* that a task produces for you personally after you've completed it. So an A represents your Gain tasks, the most significant result-producing tasks that you will ever accomplish or experience in your life. They are based on results, not deadlines. When you look back on your life on your 100th birthday, you will remember your A tasks.

Both B and C are "have to," or Prevent Pain, tasks that someone—or something—will bring to your attention if you don't do them. Both can have urgency attached to them, but here's the difference: someone, somewhere is keeping track of *if and when* you complete a B task. In other words, you not only have to complete a B, but you have to do it *well* or *on time* because it is being documented. For example, handing in your monthly report at work is a B; people will notice whether or not you did it on time. Sending invoices or ordering inventory on time is a B because it will be tracked and used in your performance appraisal. Another example is paying your mortgage or credit card bills, because credit bureaus are tracking whether or not you do that on time. In contrast, no one is keeping track of how well you complete a C task. Anyone who would keep track of how well you take out the trash or check your e-mail has too much time on his hands.

The old maxim that "whatever gets measured, gets done" has been attributed to many different authors and thinkers over the years. It essentially means that if you are in a management position and you want your employees to complete something, then you need to measure it, track it, require that it be done by a certain time, and then record performance surrounding it. In other words, if you communicate standards clearly, then they will be reached. This is true as long as what's measured *makes sense*. But another maxim, which has been attributed to Albert Einstein, goes like this: "Not everything that can be counted counts, and not everything that counts can be counted." This should speak to organizations as they determine what they need to measure and record and as they set metrics accordingly. However, as far as prioritizing is concerned, once the metric has been set, the task becomes a B for everyone who needs to follow it, because it is recorded and it affects performance ratings. You raise the priority of work that you delegate to others by keeping a record.

I once worked for a company where a C on everyone's list—in this case, attending a weekly meeting—quickly turned into a B. I was in charge of the agenda for the weekly staff meeting. I would begin the meeting by reading over the agenda that the department director had handed down to me and then assign work items to be completed during the week to meet project goals. Everyone in the department was supposed to attend the meeting.

If you are rolling your eyes as you read this, then you have probably been to meetings like this and know all about them. No one wants to go to these things. Frequently employees would get "stuck" on phone calls and have to skip the meetings or would find some other excuse for missing them. Many would show up late to express their disdain of the process in a passive-aggressive way. And although I didn't enjoy it either, it was my job to get everyone there.

So I had an idea.

One week, I secretly wrote down the exact time that each person walked through the meeting room door and said nothing about it to anyone. I went about the meeting as usual. The following week I opened the 10 AM meeting with a quick slide that showed each person's name and the time he or she arrived at the previous meeting. You can imagine the shock on people's faces. I showed the slide exactly at 10:00 and left it up only for a few seconds. I wasn't trying to embarrass anyone; I just wanted to get my point across. Of course, because it was only 10:00, many people—the chronic latecomers—hadn't arrived yet. As they trickled in, the looks they were getting from the people in the meeting who had seen the slide must have been very confusing to them.

The buzz about "the slide" got around quickly enough, because by the following week's meeting, everyone arrived on time. Most people were even early and ready to start at exactly 10:00. I have to admit I laughed to myself about it for days. But the biggest benefit was not my amusement; it was that *my* director was measuring *my* metric of getting everyone to the weekly meeting—and *now* it was getting done. As an added bonus to everyone, the meeting lasted only 20 minutes, because everyone was there on time ready to listen and get back to work when it was over.

The weekly meeting was a C, a Prevent Pain task that no one enjoyed, a "have to" on the to-do list. But by adding a recording of their performance—their attendance and arrival time—it immediately became a B, something that could come back to them later in a performance appraisal, annual review, or even just on "the slide" the following week. As the saying goes, whatever gets measured gets done.

So there are important recorded "have to" tasks (Bs), and there are unrecorded "have to" tasks (Cs). As we discussed in Chapter 1, you have to do these Prevent Pain tasks if you want to be in the game of life, even though these are things you don't remember doing when you look back on your life.

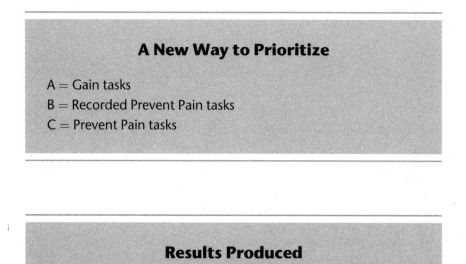

A New Way to Prioritize

A = Gain tasks
B = Recorded Prevent Pain tasks
C = Prevent Pain tasks

Results Produced

A = Goals, leadership, improvement
B = Important maintenance responsibilities
C = Maintenance

Think about the trash example: in this new model of prioritizing, would taking out the trash get an A, B, or C in priority? It would always be a C, no matter how soon the truck is coming down the street—because if you don't do it, a family member or even a neighbor will tell you to get rid of the smell coming from your trash cans! A Prevent Pain task like taking out the trash would never get an A in our new approach, because it doesn't produce significant results in your life. And it wouldn't get a B because no one is recording it. Your performance evaluation of life doesn't depend on getting it done. Completing it just gives you the illusion of productivity—and the biggest obstacle to *actual* productivity is the *illusion* of it. The first step to being truly productive is getting an accurate picture of what results each task produces and acting accordingly. Although there will still be times when you have to run after the trash truck, don't fool yourself into thinking that you checked off an A on your list in doing so.

Always remember the second attribute of Gain tasks: you don't have to do them. They're the activities in your life that produce the most significant and satisfying personal results, the things that give you your identity. These are the memories, outcomes, feelings, progress, growth, and improvement in your life—the things we remember for a year, five years, a decade, or a lifetime. Then there are things that we don't remember 5 minutes after we do them but to which we often give a higher priority than we give our A-level tasks. We allow this to happen by making sure that we do those insignificant things on a regular basis, and we can go for years without doing anything about our goals.

This new approach requires us to draw a line in the sand. We're giving your Gain tasks an A, and your Prevent Pain tasks a B or C. We are prioritizing in relation to *results*.

WHY IS PRIORITIZING IMPORTANT?

This is, of course, a reversal of conventional thought on prioritizing, because we're giving top priority to things that you don't have to do, and making things you have to do medium or low priority. This seems like another inherent discord between where our time has to go and where we want it to go, and that's why prioritizing is so important. If we don't recognize and act upon what is most meaningful to us, we will never get to the "want to" part of life.

Have you ever listed all of the Prevent Pain tasks that you have to complete on a regular basis? Here is a sample list that participants in my presentations have brainstormed. Consider how much time you spend on these in every 24-hour period. Some people have more responsibilities in some areas than others.

Prevent Pain Task Examples

Taking out the trash	Getting a haircut	Exercising
Paying bills	Doing taxes	Doing laundry
Caring for pets	Attending events	Grocery shopping
Spending time with friends/neighbors	Finding lost things	Commuting/driving
Fixing broken things	E-mailing/reading or writing regular mail	Going to the cleaners
Going to the bank/ATM	Housekeeping/cleaning	Caring for and maintaining the car
Daily personal grooming	Caring for and maintaining the lawn	Seeing the dentist/doctor
Planning parties & celebrations	Answering/replying to phone calls	Shopping for clothes, necessities, and gifts
Taking care of/spending time with family	Preparing, eating, and cleaning up after meals	Doing home maintenance, repairs, and projects
Serving as a taxicab for others (kids, friends, etc.)	Succumbing to and recovering from Illness or Injuries	Consuming information (learning, updating, waiting for, looking for, researching)

FIGURE 3.1

Do you notice what's missing from this list? What do most of us do at least 8 hours per day: *work!* Some components like voice mail and e-mail are listed, but those things exist in our personal lives as well. What about the routines of the workday that you do every day?

What else is missing? It's something else many people do 8 hours per day (although some aren't so lucky): *sleep*. Work and sleep are probably the two most time-consuming things that we do! All of this other stuff is crammed into the remaining hours of the day.

Take a long look at Figure 3.1. This is your life outside of work and sleep every day!

Some people might wonder why *family* is on a list of "have to" tasks. But think about people with aging parents or other dependent family members who need care. Even if you don't have those kinds of responsibilities, you probably still have to call your mother or brother once in a while to say, "Hi, I'm still alive! I'm over here Preventing Pain every day!" The same thing is true with friends. Favors are asked, and time is given to friends or neighbors in need. With relationships sometimes come obligations out of love and respect, companionship and loyalty, fairness and reciprocity.

There are even times at work when you walk around thinking, "Who do I owe?" Let's say you have an afternoon meeting with four people. What do you spend the entire morning *before* that meeting doing? Getting back to every e-mail and voice mail that pertains to those people! Because if you don't, the first thing you will hear when you walk into that meeting is, "Hey, did you get that e-mail I sent you last week?" She knows you got it, and *you* know you got it—but you didn't respond, so guess what? You have to deal with the pain part of the Prevent Pain that you didn't prevent! You now have to face the consequences of failing to do what someone expected you to do, and as a result, you have to repair the trust that has been broken, get over the embarrassment that you feel, and restore the confidence that has been lost. That's going to be even more trouble than just doing the Prevent Pain task in the first place!

FOCUS ON RESULTS

Failing to complete Prevent Pain tasks can produce significant *negative* results, whereas *doing Gain tasks* produces significant *positive* results. If you do not complete your Prevent Pain tasks and obligations, then you will eventually suffer negative consequences for failing to live up to your responsibilities. However, if all of your pursuits are in the Prevent Pain category and none are in the Gain category, you will continue getting the same results you are producing now without ever progressing forward. You will be standing still in the same place for years to come. Perhaps you are in a great place in your life and that's fine! But there's no movement, and as we discussed, over time stagnation leads to decay and burnout. The only way to produce significant positive results in your life, to move your life forward and improve the control you have over your life, is to pursue Gain. Figure 3.2 illustrates the results that Gain and Prevent Pain activities produce.

Where are you on the results continuum?

When you are producing great results in your life, you are doing things you *don't* have to do—and you are in control of your life's path. So why don't we pursue things like this every day?

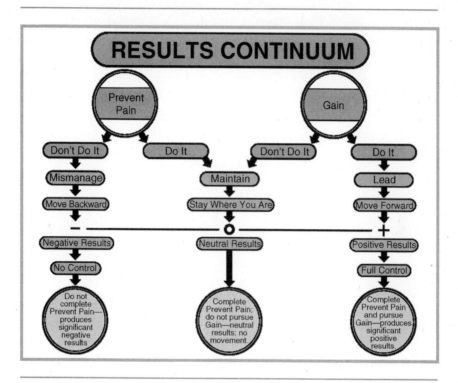

FIGURE 3.2

Because life doesn't happen in neat rows on a chart with everything you have to do listed for you and time allotted to get to each one and time left over to pursue Gain. Life happens more like this: you wake up and this is your brain:

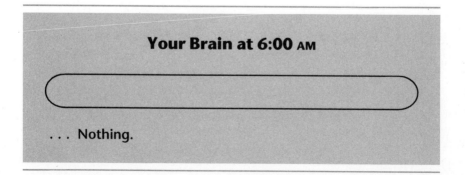

There's nothing there. Then, a few minutes into your morning, you remember you have to call John back. And you start the conversation with yourself.

Okay, remember to call John. As soon as I get to the office I'll leave him a voice mail.

Call John, don't forget to call John.

Then 2 minutes later you remember your monthly report is due.

Why do I have to do this every month? Okay, whatever—call John, monthly report, call John, monthly report.

Then you go downstairs for breakfast and it hits you . . . milk!

I forgot to pick up milk! Okay, big day, call John, monthly report, milk . . . call John, monthly report, milk.

And then before you know it, more and more Prevent Pain tasks start coming into your consciousness until your brain looks more like what's shown in Figure 3.3.

FIGURE 3.3

There you are . . . and it's only 7:00 AM! Have you ever said hi to someone and that person doesn't say hi back? You pass someone on the street or in the hallway at the office and say, "Good morning!" and you get nothing in return but a blank stare. *This is what was going on in that person's brain!* It's not that the person isn't friendly; the person is just busy thinking "John, report, milk . . . John, report, milk . . . if I say hi to you I could forget the milk! You're less important than milk!"

The reason most people never get to their goals or their Gain tasks is because their to-do lists look like Figure 3.4.

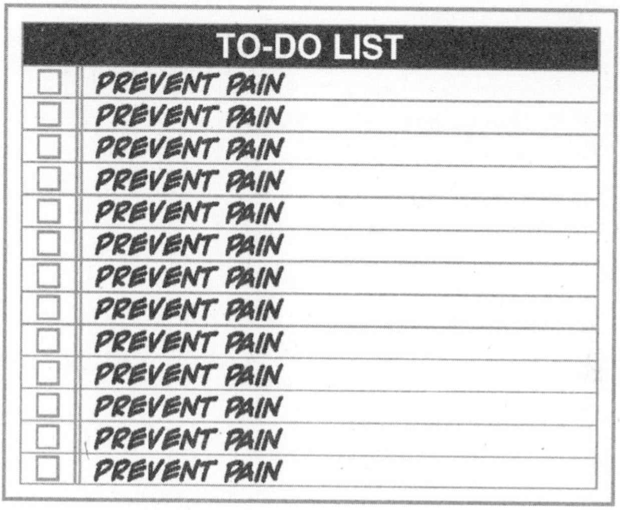

FIGURE 3.4

And this is precisely why trying to do all of your Prevent Pain tasks before you get to Gain doesn't work: *they never go away.* You need to constantly address them again and again. You can't check off getting gas for your car. Once you've done it, it just goes back to the bottom of the list, only to return in another week or so. You can't check off grocery shopping because every time you eat you are getting closer to doing that task again. Prevent Pain tasks will never go away, so staying focused on them will exhaust you. You, of course, have to get all of the Prevent Pain things done, but there's a key to successfully using your time. In the middle of a Prevent Pain day, you have to stop and do a 10-minute activity or task that moves you closer to your goals. You have to keep *moving toward Gain*.

You've likely had days when you felt like you couldn't have been busier but somehow got nothing accomplished. Those are Prevent Pain days, like the one described earlier. But the option that follows is much better. Figure 3.5 demonstrates what it looks like when you can say you had a great day, a day that moved you forward, that made your life a little better today than it was the day before.

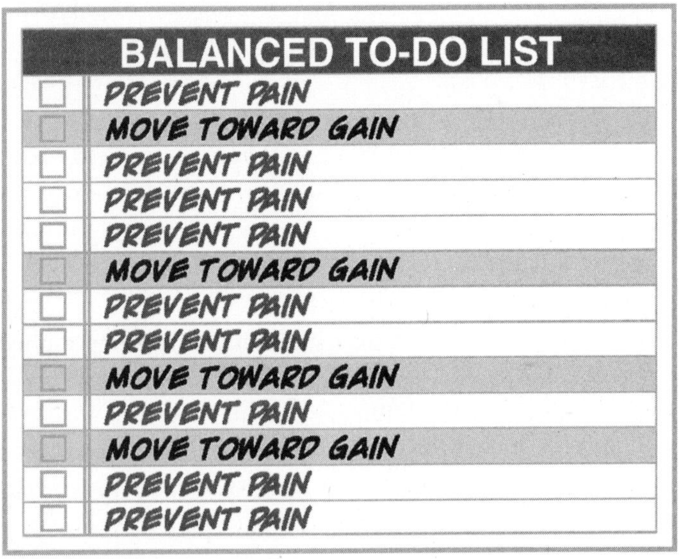

BALANCED TO-DO LIST

- [ ] PREVENT PAIN
- [ ] MOVE TOWARD GAIN
- [ ] PREVENT PAIN
- [ ] PREVENT PAIN
- [ ] PREVENT PAIN
- [ ] MOVE TOWARD GAIN
- [ ] PREVENT PAIN
- [ ] PREVENT PAIN
- [ ] MOVE TOWARD GAIN
- [ ] PREVENT PAIN
- [ ] MOVE TOWARD GAIN
- [ ] PREVENT PAIN
- [ ] PREVENT PAIN

FIGURE 3.5

If you try to finish all of your Prevent Pain tasks before you pursue Gain, then Gain will never happen, because Prevent Pain is *never* finished. You have to do both in conjunction with each other.

SURVIVAL INSTINCTS

Why don't more people manage their lives this way? There are two main reasons.

First, the brain doesn't work like a balanced to-do list, because it doesn't like to switch back and forth. Your brain is hardwired to prioritize survival over improvement, Prevent Pain over Gain, "have to" over "dont have to." It's primal. For millions of years, humans woke up and asked, "What do I have to do to survive today? Hunt? Gather? Fend off predators?" This is the same instinct that makes you think of your own survival, not just in terms of food and water, but also regarding what you have to do to get by in your life today.

This is a very difficult urge to fight. Your brain is not necessarily a mechanism designed for success, fulfillment, happiness, and growth; it is a mechanism designed for survival. It will therefore always follow that instinct and attend to what you need for protection and survival *first*. To take risks and make choices that lead to Gain, you have to override your brain's instinct and put off survival tasks in order to move forward. The good news is that once you have done this, your brain will protect these new tasks as well—and it will do what it needs to do to survive at that *new* level. But you have to break out of the constraints that you instinctively follow; you can't give your brain the choice. If you let your brain follow its instincts and deal with whatever comes to you, you are about to have a Prevent Pain day.

The second reason we don't see many people pursuing a good blend of Gain and Prevent Pain together is that even those who *do* plan, don't *prioritize* their plan effectively. They plan their Prevent Pain tasks first, thinking they will do what they have to do. Then they'll get to their Gain tasks and move toward their goals if there is any time left. But as you know, the list of Prevent Pain tasks never ends; there will always be some mundane chore that will put your Gain tasks on the back burner.

It happens like this: You start out with good intentions. You say to yourself, "If I could just get the plan for the new website started today, it would be the best day! I have been wanting to get started on that for so long, and today is the day! . . . Let me just check e-mail and see if anything came in before I get started." I've done it many times; haven't you? Do you know what you just did? You made a bad decision. You decided to Prevent Pain instead of pursue Gain—*again*. You just said, "Starting my new website would produce great results . . . but I'm going to check e-mail and see what everyone else wants me to do today instead." We can't really manage *time itself*. Time ticks on no matter what we decide to do with it. We can only manage our *decisions*.

Another reason this approach doesn't work is because Prevent Pain tasks deplete our energy. Think back to Figure 3.1; completing the chores listed in the figure is a *use* of energy, not a *source* of one. With each hour of "have to" that goes by, you feel more drained and move more slowly.

However, inserting a Gain task in the middle of a Prevent Pain day can give you the energy you need to move forward and make the Prevent Pain tasks take less time through motivation.

For example, have you ever noticed how productive you can be the week before vacation? What happens there? You work until you feel so burned out that you need and deserve a great vacation, so you plan one. Then as the date approaches you are so excited and energized by the Gain that is coming your way that you can conquer anything. You sail through those Prevent Pain tasks and even projects that have been sitting for months with no problem, because you know that you don't want to be thinking about all the little things that are waiting for you to do at work or at home when you are on vacation. You want them out of the way so you can truly relax and experience what you *want* to do. That vision gives you the energy you need to complete all your Prevent Pain faster.

Going on vacation is an easy example here, because the anticipation and excitement are obvious sources of energy and the Gain is evident and immediate. But what about other types of goals, those that might be more difficult to attain, such as writing a book? Learning a language? Opening your own business? Inventing a new product? These goals are longer term and obviously require more hard work, discipline, and focus. They can be tedious and difficult. There can be failure and repeated attempts involved, all of which sound like energy *killers!* There is certainly delayed gratification involved if you were to reach one, unlike a vacation where the whole experience is Gain from the beginning.

So the next thing we're going to do is discuss these two different types of Gain or goals.

BREAKING DOWN GAIN: CREATION VERSUS CONSUMPTION

The two types of Gain affect your motivation differently than Prevent Pain.

As you know, Gain tasks and activities are movement toward improvement that bring your life forward. However, as you have seen in the examples given, there are two types of goals: consumption goals and creation goals.

Consumption goals are things such as vacations or an occasional extravagant (but well-deserved) purchase, such as an expensive meal or luxury watch. These are fun; everyone needs some of these goals. They are worth working for, and they give life little highs to balance out the lows. They are something to celebrate and are a healthy source of short-term energy. You can often endure a particularly arduous day at work when everything seems to be going wrong by thinking about something pleasant that's coming later, such as going out to a nice dinner or even something as small as putting your feet up and watching your favorite TV show that night.

After you reach a consumption goal, you should ask yourself: Are you glad you did it? Or do you feel that you have wasted time or money? A great vacation where you recharge and encounter new people and experiences is never a waste of time. However, an extravagant vacation that you know you cannot afford but put it on your credit card anyway is not something that will bring you relaxation and renewed energy, or even peaceful memories. Having a favorite TV show to watch with a friend is a fun tradition to look forward to. However, if you feel that you waste time watching too much meaningless TV and never do anything momentous in your life, then you need to make some changes.

The difference between working hard and saving money for a certain reward and regularly binge purchasing or overindulging is *how you feel about it*. People frequently use consumption goals (for example, rewards of vacations, new clothes, electronics, or other purchases) as therapy for the burnout and depression that result from being in a rut. Consumption goals *are fun*; most of the time, they're well deserved and even necessary. But although they may bring you a reprieve from the demands of preventing pain, they are not going to make you feel like you've progressed from where you were yesterday or last year. They are only a temporary source of energy that will be depleted as soon as they are over and you return to your Prevent Pain lifestyle. If they are your only type of goal, then you are unlikely to get out of the rut you are currently in. You may even experience additional feelings of guilt for creating debt or wasting precious time.

Think of consumption goals as a *short-term reward* for the hard work you have done. You can use them as a source of energy and an incentive to get through the day, week, or month. But you need to balance them with *creation* goals, objectives that are more meaningful and that will enhance your life in the longer term.

> **We need both consumption and creation goals in our lives to feel balanced and to battle burnout.**

Creation goals are the kinds of things you wrote down at the end of Chapter 1. If you reached these goals—be it in 1 year or 5 years or 10 years—your life would be different and better than it is today. These include things such as getting a promotion, earning a higher education degree, opening your own business, repairing significant relationships, becoming involved in a volunteer group, forming new relationships for social or networking purposes, designing a new outdoor landscape or indoor living space for your home, or simplifying your life from physical, mental, or emotional clutter. Goals are incredibly unique; whatever would move your life forward and make it better for you tomorrow than it is today is a creation goal. For example, writing this book is a major creation goal for me.

The difference between these two types of goals is the impact they have on your life. Creation goals have a lasting, longer-term impact; you will remember them as being significant. Although fun and uplifting, consumption goals have a more fleeting impact.

Next we will look at how these two types of goals create and use energy in different ways and how we get the energy we need to pursue these goals and to do our Prevent Pain tasks.

Chapter 4 Energy and Motivation
Decide How You Will Get Yours

It is our choices, Harry, that show what we truly are, far more than our abilities.

—Dumbledore, from *Harry Potter and the Chamber of Secrets* by J.K. Rowling

All tasks and pursuits require energy, and not just the physical energy that keeps your body moving, but also the motivation required to focus and see projects through to fruition without becoming frustrated or distracted or giving up.

We draw on different sources of energy for the different combinations of things that we do each day. Whether we are fulfilling physiological needs, preventing the pain of consequences, or working toward rewards and results, our bodies and minds work in conjunction with each other to *push* or *pull* us forward through each day. We use these needs, consequences, and rewards as motivators to work or take action.

We are all familiar with motivation from the moment we're born, thanks to our physical needs. As stated earlier, humans are inherently driven to ensure survival. Because these basic needs never go away, motivation in its most basic form is a part of daily life. But because, as modern people, we no longer have to hunt and gather all day to ensure our survival, we have leftover motivation, a desire to want or be more in some way, and this motivation can be applied to other things. It's not just money and success, although these things do motivate many people. Motivation exists when there is a distance between where you are and where you want to be. We might want more freedom, more control over our own lives, more knowledge, more respect, or more security. Although the unique motivators evolve as we make our way through life, want different things, and identify opportunities for Gain, the process of motivation is a part of us. We are built to constantly seek satisfaction and improvement in our lives. We discussed in Chapter 2 how we suffer when this is missing or stifled in some way; that's when we start to see the effects of burnout and depression. Life is balanced only when we feel the motivation to *move* and when we have identified something to move toward.

Some people say, "I am very happy just the way I am! I don't chase bigger, better, more; I am content with life and enjoying every minute of it!" I say, well then, that's great! But what do you do with your time? In *what ways* do you enjoy life? Do you explore your creativity? Do you travel? Do you devour books or media on topics that intrigue you? Do you volunteer to help those less fortunate? These are all things you are motivated toward. All these things represent Gain, growth, and movement—in your own unique direction. It's not about chasing more money and success; it's about our motivation to continue to grow, develop, and evolve.

Motivation is fundamental to our survival and an innate part of who we are. So after satisfying our most basic and strongest needs, we still have motivation that gives us energy. We have instincts to maximize pleasure and well-being and minimize pain beyond the physical sense; this is the direction toward which we turn our energy after our survival needs are secured.

We therefore shouldn't waste such a strong force by performing only menial chores such as taking out the trash and showing up for work on time. To explore how we can use our motivation to not only complete our Prevent Pain tasks but also move toward Gain, it might be helpful to take a look at how our brain chemistry—and its mission for survival—can also help us thrive along the way.

WHAT CAN YOUR BRAIN DO FOR YOU?

There is, of course, complicated neuroscience behind how brain chemistry works, but to discuss it on a very basic level, these chemicals do things like help us overcome obstacles and persevere on tasks, condition us to seek rewarding behavior, and encourage us to muster up energy.

This need for motivation and perseverance is basic to our survival. When our ancestors needed to work all day to hunt and gather food, find shelter, or run from predators, they needed their body chemistry to cooperate and work *with* them, not *against* them. I doubt that lazy or easily distracted cavemen could have lived too long. They had endorphins working for them to help mask pain and enable them to continue fighting to survive. They had dopamine and serotonin conditioning them to repeat behaviors that led to rewards. And their adrenaline gave them the ability to jump into action and fight or flee if a threat was near.

The funny thing is that early humans didn't have neurobiological and psychological studies to tell them *how* to use these tools or to explain how the brain functions with or without these chemical rushes. They just used what they had to survive, and survival was all that mattered. They didn't view that as a mediocre way to live; it was simply their only goal. Their motivation to live and survive was an innate driving force, and they had the tools they needed to achieve it.

We still have these tools today, and we also have a lot more knowledge about them, thanks to a few centuries of studies and advancements in psychology and biology. Yet we still use them in much the same way: by subconsciously tapping into them when we need motivation, energy, and focus.

For example, dopamine is a naturally occurring brain chemical that enables us to recognize pleasure and happiness. Its levels increase when we receive a reward for a given activity, which conditions our brains to repeat these reward-driven behaviors over time. Again, our brain provided us with this service to aid in survival. It helped us learn what techniques worked best for hunting, finding food, and escaping predators. We could then call on this knowledge day after day to complete all these activities more efficiently. Modern studies with lab animals have been conducted to illustrate dopamine's effects; the studies report that dopamine depravation is so detrimental that it caused the animals to lose their motivation to eat, despite nearly starving. Without this helpful chemical we wouldn't know what behaviors to perform to get what we want.

Endorphins, for which there are both natural and artificial sources, work hard for us as well. Do you ever include an item you've already completed on your to-do list just so you can check it off? Making a long list of "have to" stuff can be uninspiring, to say the least. But checking off already completed tasks gives us the sense that we've accomplished something. We get a little lift—and experience a push toward progress. It's a little trick we play on ourselves to try to get a small burst of positive motivation and a rush of endorphins to make us want to get started on the next thing.

Endorphins are built-in painkillers that your body produces in response to stress, fear, pleasure, pain, excitement, or other stimuli. Their natural purpose is to mask pain and enhance feelings of euphoria and well-being, enabling you to keep going. This is a primal throwback to the fight-or-flight response to threats. Endorphins enable us to temporarily overcome obstacles (such as pain and exhaustion) to do whatever task is at hand, similar to having the ability to run from predators over long distances. These pain-masking and euphoric feelings that our bodies are trained to produce can be mimicked by artificial sources of endorphins, including drugs and alcohol. However, these artificial sources carry the added danger of addiction and toxicity, and with continued abuse, they impede the body's ability to produce the *natural* kind. This is dangerous, because once the ability to produce natural endorphins is diminished, dependence on the artificial kind is increased. This is how a cycle of dependence on the artificial sources results.

The good news is there are many natural ways to get the endorphins we seek without artificial sources. In addition to aiding us in primitive survival, natural endorphins have been proved to be released in response to such common physical stimuli as exercise, consumption of hot chili peppers or chocolate, romance, acupuncture, and exposure to real or artificial sunlight, as well as thrills such as riding roller coasters and mental stimuli such as attention from others, recognition, laughter, competition, or (most relevant to our topic) *a sense of accomplishment*. Completing a task of any size or importance gives us that little surge of energy and enthusiasm from accomplishment. The more important the completed task, the happier, more confident, and more powerful we feel.

The endorphin release is a positive experience that we humans *like*, prompting us to repeat the activities, tasks, or experiences that produced it. Endorphins can create a sense of enthusiasm and well-being from simply *anticipating* something pleasurable, such as how we feel right before we take a vacation. They make our tasks seem easier and our work less burdensome; a journey or task that starts out as arduous and insufferable gets easier as the finish line approaches, and the last leg usually brings us a burst of energy—thanks to endorphins—that carries us through.

When we are experiencing any kind of pain—physical, emotional pain, even unpleasant mental states such as boredom and distraction—the brain seeks endorphins to reproduce that painless feeling. That's when we find ourselves drifting toward thoughts of rewards and endorphin-producing stimuli.

We can draw on the positive feelings endorphins produce to help us persevere and keep moving toward Gain, despite the challenges we face along the way.

If we consider dopamine and endorphins as offense, the things that compel us to satisfy our needs, we can then consider adrenaline defense. Our bodies produce adrenaline to get us to safety when threats appear. It is the classic fight-or-flight response to fear or danger. It's another survival tool and one we're meant to use in emergency situations. However, some people find it to be so effective and exhilarating that they find ways to seek it often, even via potentially dangerous activities such as BASE jumping or skydiving.

The offensive and defensive purposes of these chemicals are indicative of the dual purpose of our innate motivation: to maximize pleasure and seek rewards and also to minimize pain and ensure survival, that is, to seek Gain and to Prevent Pain. Our brains drive us to do both, and this *push and pull* effect motivates us each day.

Our primary motivation to survive comes quite simply from the fear of consequences. If we don't eat, run from predators, or procreate the species, we will die. Our ancestors didn't have to think about these things; they just did them instinctively. They were aware of the consequences if they didn't. We are working from the same position today when we complete our Prevent Pain tasks: fear of consequences. Fear remains a primary motivator when we think about what we "have to" do. However, because we don't really have to worry about *survival* in the same sense that our ancestors did, we have more time available and we have the capacity to think about what *else* we want to do *besides* simply surviving. Our ancestors never had time to do this. But now, we have the benefits of predictable food sources, domestication of animals, advanced civilizations, industrialization, agricultural systems, and so on. The greatest gift that all these millennia of advancements have provided us with is the opportunity to ask: What do I want to do with my life? What Gain do I want to pursue? *This is the second category of motivation: desire.*

> **The two categories of motivation are *fear* and *desire*. We *fear* the pain of consequences of not doing something we "have to" do. We *desire* the results brought on by Gain and movement in our lives.**

We draw energy from both, and we use the same tools that our brains give us to help maximize both. *We get to decide which category to work from.* And this decision is a big factor in whether we *manage* our lives and stay where we are or *lead* our lives forward and make them better.

ENERGY FROM DESIRE: CREATION AND CONSUMPTION

When we pursue a *creation* goal, that type of Gain that moves us forward on the results continuum, we start to see results, and it inspires us. The difference between this and a consumption goal is that a creation goal's reward comes *after* we've done the work. We get endorphins from the sense of accomplishment that follows our achievement of Gain tasks. We feel that the reward matched the effort, and we use that high to get through each interim step. When you know Gain is coming and your life is improving, it feels great—and it gets you through all those "have to" tasks.

The energy to do your Prevent Pain tasks comes from pursuing Gain.

We can also use the endorphins and excitement from consumption goals to fuel our creation Gain tasks. Use the energy you get from looking forward to a great vacation to motivate you to complete Gain tasks for a creation goal. This is the way to maintain a positive attitude and stay out of a rut.

Although the impact of creation goals lasts longer, not all creation goals take a long time to achieve. You can write an article you want to publish in one evening. You can spend an hour working out and feel good all day. You can attend a professional seminar to advance your skills. But if you do have a long-term creation goal to work toward, using the energy from consumption goals or interim rewards is a great way to get there.

When you have a long-term goal, it's crucial to celebrate and reward yourself along the way. If you try to wait until the whole thing is over to feel rewarded, you run the risk of being exhausted and giving up before you get there. Share your milestones with the people who want you to succeed. Use the positive energy you get from them to give you the momentum to keep going and prevent you from giving up.

Don't get so caught up in the minutia of a long-term project that you lose sight of the *destination*. Getting a college degree or professional certification is an accomplishment to celebrate, but if you wait for four years until it's over without celebrating any consumption goals along the way, you may reach exhaustion before you reach success. If you plan to run a marathon, you need to celebrate each 5k or 10k race you do in preparation of the big day, or reward yourself after every five workouts with something that makes you want to keep going. If you're expanding your business, celebrate each step along the way in order to make all the overtime hours feel less burdensome. Even if you're just tracking your progress toward a new sales goal, seeing the results can release the endorphins and give you the momentum you need to keep moving forward. Think of your significant relationships as enduring creation goals as well. These long-term commitments can get lost in the minutia of daily life if we don't take care of them. Milestone celebrations and consumption goals shared with the people in your life renew your commitment to the process and your enthusiasm for success, and they renew your energy around the goal.

Figure 4.1 shows the different ways creation and consumption goals produce endorphins.

Consumption goals do so *right away* by delivering excitement *during* the consumption while you are having fun and for a while *after* as a result of the memories you've made and relationships you've built. This is the reward that you anticipate and complete your Prevent Pain to achieve.

Researchers who conducted a study on how vacations affect happiness levels found that the biggest boost in mood occurred from simply *planning* the vacation and that levels remained high for as long as eight weeks prior to leaving. However, happiness dropped back to baseline levels almost immediately after the vacation was over. Even the few who reported

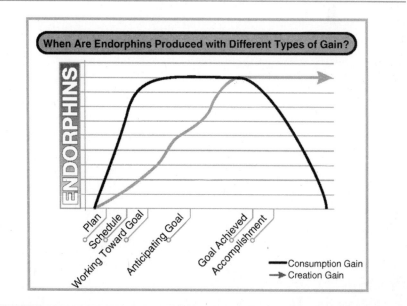

FIGURE 4.1

extraordinarily phenomenal vacation experiences showed an increase in happiness for only two weeks after the vacation. The study proved that although consumption goals do make people happy and correlate to increased productivity, the effect is felt mostly in the anticipation stage and is short lived afterward.

Of course, this is not a reason to go *without* consumption goals entirely; another study found that those who deprived themselves of vacations were more tense, depressed, and tired—and even eight times more likely to develop heart disease than those who took vacations regularly. So although the gratifying effects from consumption goals may be short lived, they are still necessary and valuable to our long-term motivation.[1,2]

The fact that gratification is delayed with creation goals makes them more difficult to initiate than consumption goals. Study hard and you'll get a good grade for the semester; work hard and you'll get a promotion. The endorphin release that you experience after achieving a creation goal—that feeling of euphoria and pride—is the reward for accomplishing something. But the creation idea of "You'll feel great *after* you do it!" doesn't persuade most people as much as the consumption idea of "You'll have fun *while* you're doing it!" That's why more people pursue Gains such as vacations, purchases, and elegant meals rather than building sweat equity to open a new business, pulling all-nighters to invent or write something new, dieting and exercising for a year to achieve a weight loss goal, putting their heart and soul into creating new art, or even taking the extra strides to improve their significant relationships and be the best spouse, sibling, parent, or friend they can be. But it's also why so many people find themselves stuck in their lives without knowing how to move forward. Consumption goals can give you only a brief reprieve before you are back to the same place in life that made you want a break. Only creation goals can move you forward out of that place.

Even though the rewards can be great, the time, sacrifice, and hard work that are often involved with long-term creation goals can be discouraging at first. For example, many years ago when my wife was considering going to graduate school at night, she lamented that it would take five years to earn a degree. A wise person posed the thought: "Five years are going to pass anyway. Do you want to still be thinking about it then, or do you want to have a degree to show for it when they're over?" In other words, time itself will not change our life situation. When five years pass, we will still be in the same place we are in now unless we put forth the effort to improve and move forward. The only difference between life standing still five years from now and achieving a great accomplishment with lifelong rewards was getting started right away and putting forth the effort. This idea was powerful to us and became a cornerstone of the way we make decisions. Time passes. If you have put forth the effort during that time to make the future better than it is today, then you can experience long-term positive results.

The results that come from accomplishing a creation goal can be enduring. Earning a college degree means you will have that degree to benefit from for the rest of your life. Receiving an award in your career means you have that award and the respect that goes with it throughout your career. Inventing a new product means that you will always be that product's inventor. Climbing a mountain or running a marathon means that you forever have that accomplishment from which you derive pride, confidence, and experience. The impact of these hard-earned accomplishments on your self-esteem and confidence can be lifelong. Conversely, as necessary as regular consumption goals are, their impact on your morale and your energy are fleeting. That's why we seek them often! The endorphin boost from consumption goals can be described as easy come, easy go, and we seek lots of little boosts like that on a regular basis to maintain satisfaction and relaxation.

The delayed rewards of creation goals may test your resolve and challenge your perseverance, regardless of whether or not you love the work involved in reaching it. But that's the nature of these tasks; if they didn't challenge you, you would have accomplished them long ago. This is the hard work from which you earn endorphins, the work that you schedule the reward for, but the pride and euphoric feelings associated with accomplishing your goal don't come until after your work is done.

So although long-term creation goals often require more energy, motivation, inspiration, work, and sacrifice to achieve, they are worthy of the extra effort because *the rewards you get from them have a longer-term impact on the quality of your life than the rewards you get from consumption goals.* This is not an either/or dilemma. Rather it is an awareness that *both* consumption *and* creation goals are necessary to feel balanced and avoid burnout, and you must understand how the rewards for each one work. You can plan to use the energy you derive from your consumption goals to not only complete Prevent Pain tasks but also *take advantage* of that boost of energy to do the Gain tasks for creation goals.

ENERGY FROM FEAR: PROCRASTINATION

Let's say you haven't completely jumped on the Gain bandwagon just yet or haven't done enough A tasks to get through your Prevent Pains today. Do some of your Prevent Pain tasks have deadlines? Are you feeling defeated or nervous as you look at the list of these tasks? Well, there *is* another way to get your energy. It's called procrastination. You are probably familiar with what is about to happen to you. You will feel an adrenaline rush very soon. This is how we get energy from fear!

Procrastination is the decision you make when you opt to draw energy from the fear of consequences instead of the accomplishment of Gain tasks. You wait until you get so close to the deadline for something that you scare yourself into thinking you might not get it done on time, and then you'll have to face the consequences. This fear gives you the burst of energy you need to do the task. The adrenaline rush it produces is the same as the fight-or-flight response to fear in our DNA. It is a stress reaction that's actually helpful for the body and mind in the short term, because it allows you to focus all your energy on the threat at hand, thereby increasing your chances of survival. And even though getting a report to your boss on time is not the same thing as running from a predator, our bodies react in much the same way. Fear propels us into action.

It's the reason why we set our alarm clocks 10 or even 15 minutes fast; that way, when we wake up, our reaction is, "Ahh! I'm late." And we get that little energy or adrenaline rush that helps us get out of bed.

Procrastination is how we use fear to do something we don't want to do.

I know you don't feel like doing it and you know you don't feel like doing it, so just wait until it's due in a half hour, then scare yourself into doing it!

Figure 4.2 illustrates the cycle of procrastination. Let's say you have a research paper due that you don't want to do. You wait until the fear of consequences thrusts you into action and finish it just in time. Then, once the fear has passed, you return to inaction and cease to be motivated. The next task comes along, and you start the cycle over again.

Many people use the procrastination of one big time-consuming task to get the energy to do other things they have been putting off instead. This is why, when you have a big monthly report due the next day, you opt to instead finish your expense report, return messages, clean your desk, and

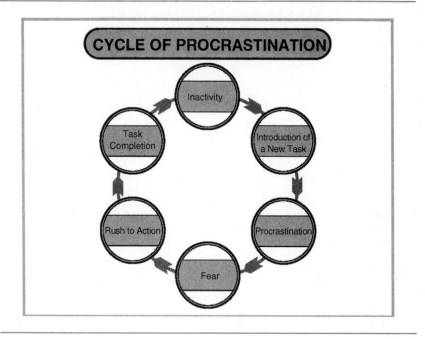

FIGURE 4.2

organize your files. If you are moving in a few weeks and have to start packing up the attic, you find yourself rearranging your sock drawer or setting up a new e-mail folder system instead.

Procrastination has gotten a bad reputation in most time management and leadership teachings—and for good reason. It is time management's biggest bad habit, usually associated with laziness, weakness, disorganization, and a lack of self-discipline. So why do we *all* do it? Well, it turns out that there are actually some *benefits* to putting off the inevitable. In some cases procrastination can do more good than harm.

Benefits of Procrastination

1. **Energy:** This is the most valuable benefit in that it enables you to do what you didn't want to do. You clearly weren't looking forward to doing this task, or you wouldn't have put it off for so long in the first place. If you wait until the fear of consequences propels you into action on a task, the adrenaline rush will motivate you to tackle the task immediately. And as everyone knows, starting a project you

don't want to do is the hardest part. If you need a wave of fear to kick you into gear and get you to jump in, then you have found it by procrastinating. And bam! You've started the task, which means you are on your way to getting it finished.

2. **Focus:** This is the second most valuable benefit of procrastination, and it is why some people *thrive* when working under pressure. Fear allows for extra strength, clear focus, and concentration on the task at hand. Adrenaline starts to rush in as you approach a deadline. Suddenly, you refuse to tolerate any interruptions or allow any outside distractions—from phone, e-mail, or visitors—until you have finished this task. Fear can wake you up and give you the kind of clarity of mind that comes from a good night's sleep or a jolt of caffeine.

3. **Speed:** If a task will take at least 1 hour for you to complete and you have exactly 1 hour left before the deadline, then there is no chance you'll waste any more time. You have not given yourself the luxury of taking a break in the middle, letting your mind wander, or giving this item more time than it needs. In 1 hour, you will definitely be able to check this off your to-do list.

4. **Less Effort:** You don't need discipline to start and stay focused on a task; the deadline and the fear of consequences will do this for you. It would have taken a lot of discipline to do that 4-hour report several days before it was due or to wake up and start cleaning out the attic right away, but now you don't need discipline; you have *fear* to motivate you instead. This is a big deal because discipline is no fun—and it's difficult! Even though it may seem like a lot of effort to work at a frenzied pace to get something done at the last minute, you have employed fear and adrenaline to get you jump started. You didn't have to muster up that energy to force yourself to start the project.

There you have it!

Now, you probably ask yourself every time you procrastinate, "Why do I do this to myself?" The answer is now clear: to *get the energy* to do the things we don't want to do. Your *energy* level heightens, you *focus* and are able to better block out distractions. Your *speed* is faster; you pick up your pace to ensure it gets done on time. And it takes *less effort*; it's easier! These are the benefits to procrastination.

Sounds good to me! Right?

This is why so many people say, "I do my best work at the last minute." Fear is an effective motivator for them. Waiting until the deadline creates an urgent environment that feels like efficiency. You complete a lot of work in a short time, so it must be good. But you're not really measuring quality; you're measuring quantity, in that at least *some* quantity of work actually got finished. Are you really producing your best work when you're that rushed? Do you create the same quality work at the last minute that you do when you give yourself the appropriate amount of time?

This brings us to the reasons why procrastination has such a bad reputation.

Problems with Procrastination

1. **Stress:** You put yourself under pressure when you procrastinate. The medical community has warned against stress and made its many health hazards abundantly clear. Although short-term bursts of energy for fight-or-flight situations were intended to aid survival, they're not meant to be sustained over a long period of time. Making a lifestyle out of procrastinating is not exactly healthy or relaxing. Stress was originally a method of survival, but we know that if you put yourself in survival mode for too long, you again face the consequences of getting burned out. How do you feel when you have been in a cycle of procrastinating and rushing to meet deadlines for a while? Run down, stressed, tired, unbalanced, defeated? That's not a sustainable method of working or managing our lives.

2. **Lower quality:** Pressure and quality have an adverse relationship. They don't like each other. When pressure goes up, quality often goes down. Have you ever seen someone choke under pressure, for example, athletes blowing the big game, proposals containing simple mistakes, people putting their foot in their mouth in interviews? How about products released under the pressure of a deadline only to be recalled for safety hazards?

   Projects or tasks completed at the last minute are often missing perspective, thought, clarity, reflection, research, and other people's input. The fear of the deadline hinders creativity and leads to narrow thinking. If you discover you need more time than you have allowed, then you are stuck with whatever quality you have produced at the time the deadline arrives. This can also impede other people's ability to do high-quality work, because they are influenced by the work that you do.

We have all seen this problem play out in business. I have seen companies send out million-dollar proposals that they completed at the last minute with the *wrong client name* on them. I have been a part of meetings that wasted the time of everyone involved because they were a last-minute attempt to get everyone together. I have seen people take legal action against companies because numbers were miscalculated in tax reports that were done at the eleventh hour.

When you wait until the last minute, you usually don't produce the same quality work you can when you give the work the appropriate amount of time. This just means that you should decide ahead of time the kind of quality you want your work to be associated with—and not let the deadline decide for you.

3. **Less control and convenience:** Procrastination also puts the deadline in charge of your life. After all, you have a choice as to when you are going to do the task, but once you reach the deadline, the choice is no longer yours. You then have to race against the clock to complete the task. You don't have the option to give anything else your attention. You must stay focused on your deadline until the task is finished.

The last minute is not usually the best or most convenient time to do a task. We listed speed as one of the benefits to procrastination because the energy and adrenaline you have produced in response to the fear of consequences can motivate you to quicken your pace and work faster. But what if doing something faster is not within your control? The task can sometimes take longer to complete than it would have if you had done it earlier.

For instance, let's say that you see the gas light on in your car and know your tank will be empty within 10 miles. Who or what is in charge of what you are doing right now? It's not you; the gas tank is in charge. So you had better start looking for the nearest gas station rather than continuing on the fastest route to your destination. However, if you had stopped yesterday when you had 50 miles to go until empty, you could have pulled into any one of the stations on your way home from work without any inconvenience.

The same goes for trying to do errands during rush hour. You will spend twice as long trying to get anywhere at that time. How about trying to get a dinner reservation on Valentine's Day? Forget it. You will likely call 20 restaurants before stopping for takeout on your way home from work (and dealing with the consequences).

Or have you ever tried to complete a work project at the last minute only to discover that you need critical information from someone who is on vacation that day? If you have ever done this, you are probably recoiling right now as you remember the embarrassment. There is no way to hide the fact that you procrastinated and didn't respect the project enough to give it the time, attention, and thought that it required.

When you wait until the last minute, you relinquish your ability to choose the most convenient and quickest amount of time for a task to take. You give up control over the situation and essentially roll the dice as to whether the stars will align so that you can get your tasks completed on time. This conundrum can have serious implications in business as well as your personal life.

THE FINAL JUDGMENT ON PROCRASTINATION

Now that we've weighed the benefits and problems with procrastination, it's time for the final judgment: when quality doesn't matter, it's okay to procrastinate. The quality of many Prevent Pain tasks, such as checking voice mail, filing, grocery shopping, doing the laundry, or taking out the trash, is not affected at all by doing them at the last minute. There is no reflection, analysis, research, feedback, brainstorming, deductive reasoning, or deep thought required. So use that burst of energy and focus from procrastination to get through your Prevent Pain or C tasks! No one is judging how *well* you take out the trash; it only matters that you did it. And as long as the bills get paid before they're due, then you're okay. Let the fear of missing a deadline thrust you into action to get through the meaningless "have to" things that you can't muster up the energy to do.

The problem with chronic procrastinators is that they procrastinate *everything*: A through C tasks. And procrastination doesn't work when something will be recorded—or memorable. You will wind up regretting that you waited that long and had to put your name on something that isn't up to your standards. *You can't use fear as your motivator when quality matters.* Fear is an effective motivator but ceases to motivate us after the consequences have gone away. And the stress that it causes is exhausting and can steal more energy than it creates. Think about it: How do you feel after a full day of rushing and knots in your stomach, worrying you might miss a deadline? You hardly want to do more than sit and watch TV or maybe you just want to take some headache medicine and go to bed. How does that affect your home life? You're probably not very pleasant to be around after a day like that—and you are on your way to serious burnout.

If fear is your chosen source of energy, then you have to continually procrastinate and scare yourself again and again. This is how people get into cycles of procrastination and rushing and stress that seem to go on forever and become a lifestyle. They don't know how to motivate themselves into action any other way.

When we behave in a *reactive* manner, with a flurry of activity right before the deadline, the stress and urgency are high, the quality is mediocre or lower, and the deadline is in control. (See Figure 4.3.)

But when we attack in a *proactive* manner, stress and urgency are low, quality can be as high as you can possibly make it, and you are in control. (See Figure 4.4.)

When quality matters, you need to derive the energy you need to get the work done from something other than fear, a more sustainable

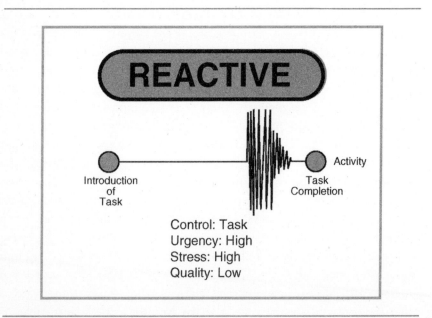

Control: Task
Urgency: High
Stress: High
Quality: Low

FIGURE 4.3

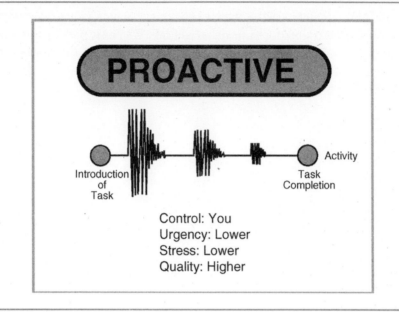

Control: You
Urgency: Lower
Stress: Lower
Quality: Higher

FIGURE 4.4

energy source, specifically, the Gain in your life. Gain continues to motivate and inspire always. Chronic procrastinators who live by deadlines *are giving up Gain*—the things they really want in life—because Gain tasks don't have deadlines or consequences if you don't do them. They are always thinking *have to, have to, have to*, and never get to *want to*.

Waiting for fear to motivate us is a reactive model of behavior instead of a proactive one. Instead of living by, "I do my best work at the last minute," why not take the approach, "I do my best work when I decide my best work is needed"—and save the last minute for stuff that doesn't matter so much? Do the important project first and then use the energy you get from accomplishing that to get through your C tasks.

Procrastination is not as much of a *time management* problem as it is a *decision-making* problem. If you *decide* to do the important, recorded, or memorable stuff, you will reduce stress, improve quality, and regain control over your time and your life. If you decide to get to the Prevent Pain tasks before the deadline, then you will also save yourself from stress and rushing and will regain control over your time.

The next chapter explores why it's so crucial to have control over your time and what it does for your quality of life. We cover the key to taking control of your time and discuss how to put an end to inappropriate procrastination, stop the reactive lifestyle, reduce stress, and make sure you have enough time to get to Gain.

Chapter 5 What Understanding the Value of Time Can Do for Your Life

Begin doing what you want to do now. We are not living in eternity. We have only this moment, sparkling like a star in our hand and melting like a snowflake.

—Sir Francis Bacon

Looking at a calendar has always made me feel more inspired than I do when just thinking about the day ahead of me. I see the dates listed and the number of blocks drawn for the week or the month for what they represent: a finite period of time with a definite beginning and end. This visual makes me realize that once I reach the last date, I will turn the page over—and never return. Whatever I have used those dates for, whatever I have experienced during that time, is, for better or worse, gone forever—and with it, the opportunities it held. And thinking about it this way compels me to make it worthwhile.

Perhaps it's becoming more apparent to me as I get older that my life is a compilation of these pages. They represent everything I did, saw, felt, accomplished, affected, influenced, thought, learned, and succeeded and failed at during that time. Every interaction with friends, family, acquaintances, clients, neighbors, and strangers that took place during that time period is now a part of my relationships with those people, for better or worse. It makes me want to approach every one of those encounters with care, to treat them as if the memory of them will last forever and cannot be changed—because it can't.

That's the thing about time. It moves in only one direction: *forward*. It is one of the rules of life that so fascinates people. Countless imaginative people have made movies and written books about getting a second chance, a do-over, rewinding just a little to take back what was said, do something a little differently, prevent a tragedy, or make a perfect moment—or to freeze time altogether to make something last. We are so fascinated by the idea of traveling back or forward in time because it would change life so fundamentally.

On the other hand, there is the beauty of time's finality: the fact that nothing can change a perfect or triumphant moment or memory that is preserved forever. We can relive in memory a gold medal athlete's Olympic performance, but we can never alter it: it is a moment we can hold onto forever. A scientific breakthrough or invention would be lost forever if time could be rewound or changed, but instead it is enshrined forever in human progress because that could never happen. And a painful departing or disaster is eased only by the *passing* of time and the continuation of seasons. It is the forward motion of life and, for better or worse, that's how it works.

It is from those moments—gained or lost, perfected or ruined—that we learn to make better choices and to appreciate time's fleeting nature, specifically in terms of the opportunities we have. We learn how time translates directly to life. The further we travel down this road, the more obvious it becomes that your time *is* your life, the whole collection of what you have done with each precious moment, each day, each tick of the second hand. Life is made up of millions of seconds running one after the other. And when you appreciate this connection, you start thinking about time itself a little differently.

Many people tend to see their lives as a series of experiences from childhood through adulthood, major events such as graduating, getting married, having children, beginning careers, or moving to a new city, or perhaps even a treasured period during our youth when we spent lots of time with good friends at our favorite places. We see the mountain peaks of our lives from a distance and don't think about the minutia of daily life. This is a more reflective view and how it should be. This journey of experiences, thoughts, and growth tells the story of who we are, from where we started to where we finish.

One actual minute may count for more than another in your memory, but in actuality, one minute in time is no longer or more important than the next; each holds the same percentage of your life. Our memories give *significance* to one time over another according to what we have done with it. The minute I spent many years ago saying vows and "I do" to my wife is more significant to me and to my life than the minute I spent this morning putting my laundry away. However, both were 60-second time periods.

This is not meant to imply that putting laundry away or engaging in any other Prevent Pain task is not worthwhile. As we know, we have to complete them regularly to keep up with life. However, when we start to see that time is an immovable, unchangeable force—and that the collection of each unit of time is vital to what we eventually call our whole life—we start to see it differently.

Of course, we can't spend all our time thinking about how to make each precise minute count toward a lifetime of fulfillment. If we did, we would never finish any of the chores that keep us up to date at work and at home. This idea that time is life is not meant to pressure you into trying to do something extraordinary with the next hour. It is simply meant to make you more aware of how life has unfolded up until now and how it will continue to do so in the future. The decisions that you have made as to how to spend your time up until now have yielded the results that you have experienced and have brought you to the life you currently have.

We know that "have to" tasks are necessary to keep up with life. It is the "don't have to" tasks, the Gain or A tasks, that distinguish one person from the next, that make your life worth living and make you who you are. Have you ever heard a person described like this:

> Well, he breathes every day, brushes his teeth every day, eats every day, occasionally does laundry, shows up for work, and takes out the trash.

Wow, what a legacy. We don't describe people like that because *everyone* has to do those things. Nothing about our Prevent Pain tasks sets us apart us from anyone else. The results you get every day are not determined by the "have to" tasks.

THE VALUE OF A MINUTE

When you start to appreciate that your life is composed of each individual unit of time to use as you please, you will see that anything you are doing at any given moment in time is your *highest priority in life right now*, simply because *that* is what you chose to do with it. This is not meant to compel you to jump into action or to convince you to spend your time doing something different than what you are already doing. It's merely an observation: if you are taking out the trash right now, then taking out the trash is the most important thing you could be doing in your life *right now*. Obviously, the trash is not important to you in terms of the big picture. But when you say to yourself, "I'll take it out to the street now and get it out of here before it starts to smell," it's the best decision you could make—and the most important thing you could be doing with that minute. If it wasn't, you would have chosen to do something else and let the trash wait a little longer. As we know, even our least enjoyable and momentous Prevent Pain tasks eventually rise in urgency. It doesn't change their results; they still merely prevent pain.

But when you determine that they need your attention that minute, you've decided that doing them is currently the best way to use your time.

It's rare that we *consciously* make a decision regarding our highest priority in life right at that minute. The best we can usually do is to take a few minutes to plan out the day and, if it's a great day, keep the plan in mind as the day moves along. However, we do make countless sub-conscious decisions: work, do chores, sleep, relax, hang out, surf the Internet, catch up on social media, exercise, commute—the examples are endless. Sometimes the best use of your time is to pursue Gain, whether it's a creation goal like looking for a new job or consumption goal such as having a fun night out; sometimes the best use of your time is to prevent pain because pain is no fun.

With whatever decision you make, there is an *opportunity cost* to that choice, just as there is with your money. If you decide to spend $20 on one thing, you can't spend that same $20 on something else. Most people understand this, regardless of whether or not they adhere to it and have the discipline to stick to it. If you have $10 in your wallet and you spend it on lunch, you do not have that $10 anymore. That choice was yours to make. No one forced you to make it.

The same is true of your time. If you decide to spend your time this evening making dinner and watching a movie, then that is what you decided was the best use of your time and your highest priority that evening. However, you can't also spend that time going to bed early, visiting the gym, organizing your home office, going to a baseball game, writing a book, or climbing a mountain. You already chose what you were going to do with your time—and that choice eliminated every other option.

Perhaps you are reading this book while commuting on a train. You could be reading e-mails or looking out the window or closing your eyes and thinking about the day, but you decided that reading a book about making better decisions was the best way to use your time right now. (Good choice!) Whenever you choose to do something, you are determining, consciously or not, that this option is the best use of your time. Whether or not the choice was a *good* one is your opinion and should be based on whether or not it produced the results you wanted. If it was a good movie, or even if it wasn't but it gave you the chance to relax, then you are probably very pleased with your choice. You must *own* the decisions you make about your time before you can take control of it. And it follows that because your time is your life, you must own the decisions you make about your time before you can take control of your *life*.

Let's say you regret your decision; the movie was bad, and you didn't get to relax at all. You wish you'd spent your time or money on something else instead. Then you made a bad decision. Sometimes that happens, and we learn from it. That feeling of regret means that you didn't value what you chose as much as you would have valued something else. Ultimately, the things on which we spend our time and money are what we value. As I've said to many clients over the years: show me your calendar and your credit card statement and I'll be able to tell you what you value. Your family, home, career, hobbies, and charities are all indicative of what we hold dear. Some of them are choices we made long ago, ones that inherently bring responsibilities and Prevent Pain tasks, such as home ownership and parenting. We decided that our lives would be better if we lived in that house, had these relationships, got this job, or bought that car. Those are *decisions*. And when we see them only in terms of what we have to do to maintain them, then we need to alter either our attitude or our lifestyle and figure out how to make better long-term decisions in the future. Every action and choice has results, whether they are positive, negative, long term, or short term. When you start to own your choices, you will also own your results—and have better control over them. Taking control of your decisions is the difference between leading forward and merely managing the life that *happens to you* if you don't.

When you start to see your time as your most valuable, irreplaceable resource, you see its *worth*. What you choose to do with it reflects your priorities and directly produces the results you get. My goal is to have you see time that way. Your life is a product of all the decisions that you've made on where to spend your time—up until this point. If you understand the opportunities that time presents, then you can use it to improve your life and move it forward.

UNDERSTANDING WHERE OUR TIME GOES

To start making better decisions about our time, we need to understand what comprises our time in the first place. And we can classify pretty much everything we do every day into three categories: habits, to-do items, and calendar events.

Habits are things we spend time on that we don't have to write down or think about, because we don't normally forget to do them. They include our daily routines: sleeping, brushing our teeth, eating a meal, commuting to work, reading before bed, catching up on the news headlines on the way into work, turning on the TV when we get home. They are nonevents, conditioning, the same thing over and over again, perhaps triggered by a naturally occurring stimulus such as waking up in the morning, feeling hungry, or seeing a certain time displayed on the clock. If you know you have to leave for work by 7:15 AM every day to arrive on time, then that becomes part of your routine. It's not something you need to write down each day so you won't forget; it's a built-in part of your day.

Habits mostly influence parts of life such as hygiene, health, eating, repeat spending, relaxing, chores (for example, doing dishes), and rote tasks (such as checking e-mail and voice mail several times per day). They rely on your brain's autopilot, meaning you can concentrate on and plan other things while you are doing them. You can think about what to cover in your first meeting of the day while you are showering and brushing your teeth in the morning. You can think about what to say during a client phone call while you are commuting to work. You can watch TV while you do dishes after dinner. Even some to-do tasks reside here. You are not fully engaged in the task that you are completing; you've done it so many times that you are merely following instinct. Although habits aren't usually a big deal, they take time nonetheless. The minutes used for these things aren't free minutes that you don't count or you can get back at the end of the day. You must count habits and routines when you consider where your time goes each day.

Your *to-do list* includes maintenance tasks that you don't want to forget: updating a file, sending out a department memo, checking in with a client, sending an e-mail, submitting an expense report, going to the dry cleaners, grocery shopping, buying a gift, mailing something, paying a bill, organizing. To-do lists are for things that make you busy, that is, the mundane Prevent Pain stuff that you need to check off regardless of whether or not it has a deadline. Even if they have to get done today, these tasks are time-flexible because you don't usually assign a specific time to complete them as you would with an appointment.

The *calendar* is for things that are time-specific: events, appointments, and anything that you have to be on time for, whether it's business or personal. As a result of making something time-specific, you have to work around it and defend this time against other tasks or appointments that want the same time slot. This appointment will influence how you spend the rest of your day and where you can be before or after it. Because of the extra work involved with scheduling, working around, and defending appointments, we tend to reserve them for important things. If something inconsequential somehow makes it onto your calendar, you're apt to cancel before its time arrives in favor of anything else that comes up. You won't bother to defend the appointment and schedule around it if it's not important enough to you. Even time spent going shopping or hanging out with friends is a calendar (or scheduled) item once you have carved out and dedicated time for it.

These ways in which you spend your time account for almost everything you do each day. Is it really a part of your life if it doesn't fit into one of these three categories? Your habits, to-do items, and calendar comprise your time—and therefore your life. So how can we manage them or use them a little better to make the most out of them?

MAKE BETTER DECISIONS ABOUT YOUR TIME

Consider first whether your habits are working for or against you. Do you need to change anything about them? Is there anything you do daily that you could do better, healthier, or more efficiently? If so, changing that habit would be a great Gain task. For example, if you stopped getting fast food on your way home from work every day and started eating healthier at home, your life would probably be better tomorrow than it is today. Your first step might be to stop at the grocery store on your way home today instead. If you are satisfied with your habits and routines, then just be aware of the amount of time that you actually spend on them each day.

Make a to-do list for your daily Prevent Pain tasks so that you don't forget them and wind up procrastinating until the last minute. If you can get them done ahead of time by using your list, then you will be more in control of your time. (You may even avoid late fees on some of your bills!)

Those are the easy things to do. No one has to remind you to put a scheduled client meeting or even a dentist appointment on your calendar, because these things are fundamental; they have a trigger, a deadline, or a scheduled time. But as we know, *goals do not have these things*. Even if you've identified or written down your goals, you'll never get around to achieving them if you don't *commit to a time to work on them*. Your time will always go to other things, and you'll push them aside day after day to work on Prevent Pain survival tasks. They have no deadlines, no time when someone will come and ask, "Did you do that yet?"

You cannot accomplish A tasks, or even B tasks, on autopilot. They require your brain to do some quality thinking and *work* to get them done. Tasks like this even use a different part of your brain: primarily, the prefrontal cortex, where complex mental activity takes place. To get to that place in your brain, you have to stop thinking in survival mode.

This is where your calendar comes in. Developing healthy and efficient habits and using a to-do list are great time and life management skills, but your calendar is the tool you use to stop *managing* your life and start *moving it forward*.

YOU ACCOMPLISH GAIN BY GETTING YOUR GOALS ON YOUR CALENDAR

It's that simple.

> **The reason so many people fail to achieve their goals is because they have not committed to *defending a time* in which they will work on their goals.**

Once you set aside a spot on your calendar for working toward a goal, you won't schedule anything else during that time. Chances are that you haven't done this yet because you keep trying to *find* the time for your goals. But after working all day on Prevent Pain tasks, it's unlikely you'll say, "Hey, I have energy, I am motivated, I am thinking about my future, and I am going to improve my life!" That's usually when people lean toward consumption goals, for instance, giving themselves a fun night out, more than toward creation goals. If you've been waiting for the time to come to *you*, then stop; it hasn't happened and isn't going to. The only way to create a break in the Prevent Pain cycle is to put your goals on that reflection of what you are willing to defend: your calendar. What in life is worth defending? You wouldn't defend a task like taking out the trash because it isn't worthy of turning down other uses of your time. (See Figure 5.1.)

FIGURE 5.1

Defending time is not easy. Saying "no" to competing activities and requests to make a space for something you have scheduled is a constant reminder of how important the results you wish to Gain from that time are to you. If you have identified a worthwhile goal, then your commitment to it will grow each time you remind yourself of the results that will come from it.

What deserves that much effort to defend and plan around if not your goals? If you're going to do that much work and have the discipline to stick to it, it better be worth it in results.

Even after you've brainstormed all the Gain you can think of, if you don't put it on the calendar it won't happen. It's a matter of aligning your actions with your words. If you claim that something is important to you, then take the next step to make sure you show how important it is. If you prioritize in relation to results as we discussed in Chapter 3, you will treat your goals with the priority they deserve based on the results you know they will produce.

In essence, by moving your goals to your calendar, you are making an appointment with them. You are giving them a specific time at which you will address them in order to ensure those results. The calendar is where this process begins. It is where Gain happens.

WHY DOES THIS WORK?

Let's say that you have a dentist appointment scheduled for Tuesday at 2:00 PM, but something important comes up and you can't make it. What do you do? Most people would call the dentist's office, cancel, and reschedule the appointment during that same phone call. It would be rude to just ignore the appointment and not show up; chances are, you have a relationship with that dentist, and you wouldn't want to show him that kind of disrespect. So the simple fact that the appointment was scheduled on the calendar in the first place will make you respect it enough to reschedule it, which *keeps* it on the calendar. That appointment will keep showing up on your calendar until you make it there to see your dentist. The same is true with a Gain task. If you've scheduled it on the calendar, even if a proverbial fire breaks out at work, you can reschedule the Gain task for the next time you have available to do it. You are less likely to forget about it altogether.

Using the calendar to give your goals the attention they deserve makes the difference between *structure* and *discipline*. If you schedule time on the calendar to work on your goals, then you have to defend that time and say yes or no when it comes, giving it a better chance of getting done than if you never addressed it in the first place. If it's already an appointment on your calendar, then you have it built in to the structure of your day—and you don't need as much discipline to get it done. If it isn't on the calendar and instead is merely a dream floating around in your head or a "good idea" on a list, then you have to have discipline to make it happen. That's difficult to do when there is pain everywhere that needs to be prevented and consequences everywhere if you don't do something else. We know by now that if you put a Gain task on a to-do list right next to a Prevent Pain item, the Prevent Pain will always win, because your life is being run by habits and maintenance items. Your brain is preoccupied with survival, and survival is a never-ending responsibility. Even after you finish these tasks and are exhausted from surviving all day, finding the discipline to get up off the couch and complete a Gain task can feel difficult, if not impossible. That's why it will never work to "find time" to get to them after finishing life's maintenance work. If, however, you have an appointment scheduled on your calendar, then you can address it without as much discipline. You would schedule your day around it, put aside the Prevent Pain tasks at the time the appointment comes up, respect the appointment, and make Gain happen. There is never going to be enough time for doing what we don't have to do. It's a matter of scheduling it and respecting it. It's not *if* you have time but rather a matter of respecting it regardless of what other Prevent Pain tasks lay waiting. It's a matter of how far behind you are willing to get on your Prevent Pain tasks to pursue Gain and make more significant results happen. Let the calendar provide the discipline. If you really want to achieve your A tasks, get them off your to-do list and onto your calendar. We defend appointments. We don't defend a time-flexible to-do list.

For example, what's the first thing you'll do if I say to you, "Let's get together Monday night?" You will check your calendar to see if you have anything scheduled on Monday night. If you do, you might say, "I can't do Monday. How about Tuesday night?" We will check back and forth on our calendars to find a night that both of us are available. What just happened there? We defended whatever we already had scheduled on our calendars; we weren't checking a to-do list. We didn't say, "I have to answer some e-mails on Monday at some point, so Monday night is out." A scheduled appointment will always win against time-flexible tasks.

Using the calendar versus the to-do list affects when and even *if* we commit to things. If you asked me to send you an article we just discussed, I would *first* commit to doing it—and I would add it to my to-do list *after* I decided to commit. If you asked me to get together on Monday, I would check my calendar *first* to see if I already have any time-specific commitments that night. I would not confirm with you until *after* I checked my calendar. That's the difference in respect that we give to calendar items versus to-do items.

Why didn't I check my to-do list before I committed? Because *tasks* don't carry the same priority that *appointments* do. Tasks are time-flexible and can be moved around until such time as the deadline arrives. Appointments, however, are time-specific and are harder to move. I can e-mail an article whenever, but we have to choose a specific time to get together. You will consult your appointments before making decisions about your time. You must therefore separate survival and Gain tasks when planning. The to-do list is for your survival Prevent Pain tasks; Gain tasks belong on your calendar.

So now the question to ask yourself is, What is currently on your to-do list that *should* be on your calendar?

GETTING YOUR GOALS ON YOUR CALENDAR: THE FIRST STEPS

When you've identified a goal that's too big for you to take on all at once—as most worthwhile endeavors are—you have to break it down into interim steps.

Go back and look at your list of goals from Chapter 1. Choose the one you want to work toward, and *brainstorm* every task necessary to achieve that goal. You won't be able to think of them all at first; subsequent steps will reveal themselves to you throughout the process. As you learn more and get closer to achieving your goal, you will discover what else you might need to learn, research, or do. But you can begin by asking some basic questions and listing some fundamental steps. Your brainstormed preliminary questions might sound something like these examples.

Sample Brainstorm of Questions or Tasks Necessary to Begin Pursuing Gain

- What has to happen first?
- Are there other people involved?
- How will you find out about the process?
- Do you know anyone personally who can give you information or guidance on how to accomplish something like this?
- Can any professionals or other experienced people give you advice or share best practices?
- What resources (time, money, staff, equipment) will you need, and how can you get them?
- How long will the process take? What is a realistic time frame?

- Whose buy-in should you have: your boss's, your family's, your business partner's?
- What other stakeholders are there in this goal? Whose support do you need?
- What risks do you have to consider?
- What research do you need to do?
- Is there practice or training involved?

Because goals are so unique, not all of these questions will pertain to every goal. There will be different starting points for each goal; some will be professional while some may be personal or family- or fitness-oriented. Whatever the questions are, this is the *first* step. Begin by scheduling a short session on your calendar to brainstorm initial questions and tasks pertaining to your goal. Fifteen, 20, or 30 minutes should be sufficient depending on its complexity. Then from this list, identify the first *action step* you can take. If one session isn't enough time to do this, look at your calendar again and schedule *another* 30-minute session and see if you get farther. Once you have honed in on an initial path and action step you can take—no matter how small—*that's* the next thing you put on your calendar. Take the time to schedule it right away. Don't move on to your next appointment for the day until you have scheduled the next Gain task for that goal. Put it on the calendar for *a day this month* when you can do it. Even if it's just a 5-minute preliminary phone call or some initial Internet research, schedule it on your calendar to make sure it gets done. Then, when you have finished that task, look at your calendar and schedule the next one right away. Putting the steps that you brainstormed in order of when they should be done is flowcharting the process. It's like making a road map of how to get from here to there. Once you have an initial flowchart, you can schedule the first few steps to spark the momentum. You will naturally add or subtract a few along the way. The less intimidating your initial steps are, the more likely you are to take them. You are identifying the critical path between where you are now and accomplishing the Gain you want.

If you can get a few of these initial low-level steps under your belt, you will be on your way to taking on the more challenging steps. Your commitment to your goal will grow simply because you have *started to pursue it*—and that commitment is the most important weapon you have in your quest to accomplish it. Scheduling a single 15- or 30-minute task today can significantly move your business or your life forward, bringing you that much closer to your goal. The mere thought that you have been defending this time and will be working on Gain today will give you energy to get your Prevent Pain tasks done before and after your scheduled Gain appointment.

You *must schedule* every individual task that pertains to a goal on the calendar as a Gain appointment. When they pertain to a goal but have no deadline or defended time, these tasks are time-flexible—and will remain that way. Unless you make them time-specific, they're not going to happen.

NEED SOME EXAMPLES?

The process of brainstorming and then flowcharting a goal is critical to attacking it. Let's go through a few examples so that you can see how you might begin working on something you've long desired to do but haven't yet acted upon in any way.

Let's say, for instance, that your most coveted goal is to own an income property and rent it out to tenants. You have decided that this is a worthwhile endeavor because it will provide both an extra income stream as well as excitement and satisfaction; it will also serve as an avenue for your creativity and ingenuity if you have to fix the place up. The problem is, you don't know anything about being a landlord or managing income properties, and you have very little time to put toward this goal. As a result, you've suspended this goal for five years now. You look enviously at people who own one while you have done nothing about making it happen for yourself.

Your first step is—surprise—start brainstorming. Make a list of people who could serve as resources to you as you begin your quest. Some of these might include a real estate agent, a loan officer, a contractor, an accountant, and maybe a friend who owns an income property who could tell you the pitfalls and lessons learned along the way. Will you have a partner in this endeavor whose buy-in you'll need?

You could compile a list of information resources such as books on how to manage an income property or websites you can research. You might also collect some property value amounts for real estate in the area where you want to buy, as well as the potential rental incomes and rental histories in those areas. The next potential step would be to assess your own finances to determine how you might afford your new adventure. You might then want to start looking at listings.

This all may happen very quickly once you get started, or it may take a year or more before you find a place that makes sense to buy. One thing is for sure: it will *never* happen if you don't take the first step of educating yourself on the process.

Let's say your most coveted goal is to go to law school, because you desire the knowledge and skills that would come with a law degree. You might be looking to start a career at a law firm or just enhance your current career. But you have not been in a classroom in several years. You might start by deciding whether you want to go full-time or at night. Then, you can conduct some Internet research on the best law schools in your area that offer night classes. You can look at beginner law career opportunities and salaries for recent graduates. Then, you can research admission requirements and start looking up LSAT courses to prepare for the entrance exam. You might look at tuition help programs or student loans. Whatever your first steps are, there is a path that will get you to this goal. You just have to brainstorm and find it.

Perhaps your goal is to run for mayor or council position in your town. You have decided that this would be a worthwhile endeavor; however, you have never been involved in politics before. You might start by simply *attending* town council meetings or volunteering at town functions to see how things are run. You might want to talk to people who have run before to get their perspective on the experience. You could make a phone call to the borough office to find out what the procedure is for getting your name on the ballot. Perhaps there is a primary election you have to go through first.

Or let's say you want to open an ice cream shop. Have you ever been involved with running a food service business before—or a business of any kind, for that matter? If not, you will have to start doing some research to experience this Gain. What type of licenses or certifications would you need? How do you find out about suppliers? Do you want to own a franchise or open your own original business? How much money do you need to get started? How much revenue do businesses like this generate in similar areas? Would this be a full-time pursuit or a side business for you?

Is there anyone who has a successful business like this that has put his or her story out for others to learn from?

Finally, let's say your goal is to become a manager or reach the next level of influence in your current organization. Pursuing one of these will be a Gain task in itself, with many steps involved. Your first step is to find out whether there are any professional certifications, licenses, advanced degrees, or designations required for that level that you'll need to pursue. If those things are not necessary to advance through your organization—or if you already have what you need to do so—then a second step might be to begin talking to people who would recommend you for a management position and let them know you are interested. What books or seminars on managing might you begin researching? What newsletters, blogs, or forums on management can you subscribe to? Begin updating your résumé, portfolio, and collection of supporting documents (praise letters from clients, industry awards, performance appraisals, work samples, letters of recommendation, etc.). Work on citing and providing examples of when you improved something in your current position, thereby exhibiting true leadership. Then you need to find out what positions are available, what areas of the country you might be willing to move to for the new job if necessary, and how to apply for a position.

LEAP OF FAITH

There's still a leap of faith here. You can brainstorm it, flowchart it, put it on the calendar, defend it—and when you get to it, you still might not want to do it or be able to bring yourself to jump in and get started. Your calendar can't *do the job* for you; you are still in the driver's seat.

Things such as fear and laziness might be holding you back. You might have to move that Gain appointment around two or three times before you get tired of putting it off and are ready to give it a try. You need a little discipline to get started. This is where the brainstorming and flowcharting of interim steps help. It won't all happen at once. You don't have to say, "I'm buying an income property today, I'm going to law school today, I'm running for mayor today, I'm opening an ice cream shop, or I'm becoming a manager today." It takes much less discipline to say, "I'm making a phone call today" or "I'm doing some research today." These smaller, less intimidating steps go a long way toward building momentum around your goal, and once you start, momentum becomes something that will give you the energy you need to keep going.

If you feel that you've come to a point where you need this Gain in your life, then you *will* find the small amount of discipline necessary to take the first small steps of brainstorming and flowcharting your goal. You will honor the appointment on your calendar when it arrives. Once you are on your way, you'll feel the rush of endorphins from the sense of accomplishment of beginning your quest. And the more pride and excitement you feel, the less discipline you'll need.

This is why each person's Gain is so unique and such an individual process. A goal that someone sets *for* you does not have the same benefit or offer the same sense of accomplishment as one you've created on your own. A true goal comes from self-determination and your own desire for the experience; this is the only thing that will give it the staying power to maintain its importance to you and continue feeding the motivation by desire to achieve it. If you can't find the discipline to accomplish that first small step, your commitment to the goal is lacking. Perhaps it doesn't mean as much to you as you originally thought it did. You have to ask yourself, "How much do I *really* want it?"

There is another weapon available to you if you need it. Are you more respectful toward appointments you have with other people than you are toward appointments you have with yourself? If so, you might need to involve someone else in your appointment to make it happen, a life or career coach, a mentor, a partner or stakeholder, or a personal trainer. Even something as simple as having a friend check in on you and see if you are sticking to your Gain appointments could help. Being accountable to someone like this can make you "show up" for the Gain appointment, because you respect your relationship with that person.

It ultimately comes down to desire. Do you desire to feel balanced, satisfied, and accomplished, enough to do more than what you have to do each day to move out of a rut and lead your life forward? Do you need a change? Are you perfectly proud of where you are right now but ready to take on more? If so, then it is time to get started taking on the Gain process. Use your calendar, your flowchart, a mentor—all the weapons you have in your arsenal. You have identified a goal that would move your life forward and produce significant results, and you have divided it into smaller, manageable steps to help you get started. You have made an appointment on your calendar and defended that time so you *do* have the time to get it started. You have direction, knowledge, desire, time, and a tool (your calendar) to get you there, and you will also have momentum on your side once you get started. These weapons can be stronger than your fear or your laziness, and they can help you take that leap of faith. But you won't accomplish anything until your desire to do it is stronger than your fear of failing at it.

Does starting on the road to Gain guarantee that you will finish? Of course not. By its very nature, Gain involves risk. Perhaps your initial research will uncover that this *particular* Gain is not right for you after all, or not at this time. You might discover that it won't make your life better tomorrow, and you no longer want to pursue it. But you'll finally learn that for sure, and you can stop wondering about it and wanting it. This will give you a better idea of what direction to move toward that *would* improve your life. *Knowing what you don't want can be just as valuable as knowing what you do want.* When you stop thinking about that goal, you have more time to think about what you want. You can then use this newfound knowledge to choose a path heading in another direction.

I can't tell you whether your particular goals are worthwhile or not; only you can decide what will make your life better tomorrow than it is today. I can tell you that whatever you have chosen is what you don't have to do, and it is what will differentiate you from everyone else. These decisions—and the challenges that accompany them—will be your defining moments.

DON'T SQUEEZE IT IN

You don't have to try to fit it in today; adding more things to an already busy calendar will likely just overwhelm you. Instead, look at your calendar and see how far out you need to go before you come to a blank spot on a page. It doesn't matter how far from now that is; go out as far as you have to in order to find a time that won't make you stressed and pressed for time. You won't be able to think creatively or relax enough to think about Gain if you feel that way. Once you've identified a time, schedule your initial brainstorming session for that day. As the date approaches, you will know that you have defended time that day. Now you have that task scheduled, planned, booked—it's on there! Add one interim task from your flowchart at a time as you finish the previous one. Defending it once it's on the calendar is not as difficult as getting it on there in the first place. Let the rest of your responsibilities fill in around that priority as the date approaches, but *defend that time*.

If you don't think it's realistic to plan that far in advance, think about the other kinds of appointments you make, for instance, visiting the dentist. What's the last thing your dentist or the receptionist says before you leave the office? "Do you want to set up your next appointment for six months from now?" You made it to this appointment today, didn't you? You defended this time, set it aside, and didn't make any other appointments for this time today because you knew you had a dentist appointment. If you can make it happen for your teeth, you can make it happen for your greatest life goals. This works just as well in business. I routinely set up client engagements six months in advance, and people schedule weddings, parties, and vacations with even more notice. Defending time is just a matter of committing to what is already scheduled.

So how do you execute all of this to actually take advantage of it? Decide and commit! When you wrote down your Gain tasks in Chapter 1 (and perhaps have revised them since learning all about what Gain can do for your life), you decided what would make your life better tomorrow than it is today. Now it's time to *commit*—specifically, to two things:

1. Plan for a few minutes each day, week, and month.
2. Use your calendar as your weapon to insert Gain into your life.

The results you get from these two commitments will save you far more time than they take. They will make it possible for you to feel balanced and satisfied with your time and your decisions and allow you to start leading your life forward.

Chapter 6   Monthly, Weekly, and Daily Planning

I've always been in the right place and time. Of course, I steered myself there.

—Bob Hope

Deciding to insert Gain into your life is half the battle; now you have to commit to getting it done.

Think about all the commitments you make every day: to appointments, meetings, work projects, assignments, events, and more. You also have a commitment to yourself to survive—and to do all the Prevent Pain tasks that ensure that this happens. In return for your commitments, you get a paycheck and a life that is free of the fear of consequences. The way to make it all happen and keep those commitments is to take on one more commitment: to *planning*.

There are three levels of planning—monthly, weekly, and daily—that serve the different levels of A, B, and C tasks and activities that you do each day.

Monthly planning is for your Gain tasks—your A-level commitments. Look at the next month on your calendar and go through the brainstorming and flowcharting steps we outlined in Chapter 5 and get them on your calendar. Planning for your Gain tasks on a monthly basis allows you to see your life moving forward from a higher level than you do when envisioning each day's tasks and deadlines.

Some months will of course allow more time for Gain than others. Events such as regional meeting dates, business travel dates, doctor appointments, celebrations, vacations, and social events are usually scheduled in advance—all things you put on your calendar when you commit to them. You may see some of these things already planned when you look at the month coming up. Many industries have a busy season when they require all hands on deck for maximum productivity; during these times, you may have to put improvement on hold for several weeks. Fortunately, these are usually fairly consistent on an annual basis, so hopefully, you can plan for them in advance as well. Similarly, many people's personal lives tend to be a lot busier during the summer months, with vacations, family celebrations, parties, and get-togethers.

But seasonal trends also mean that slower periods will eventually come—when there is more time available for Gain. So *take advantage* of these times. Schedule a 30-minute time slot for a Gain task and defend it, even if it is months from now. As time goes on, other things will start to fill in around your Gain appointment—but it will be on the calendar and it will set the tone for that day. Do your monthly planning, find a blank day, and add in your Gain appointments.

Weekly planning is for your B tasks. Now that you're aware of the calendar's power to make things happen, you can use it to keep from putting off your B tasks—and ensuring they get the attention to quality they require. Take a few minutes each week to determine which B tasks you have coming up and when they are due. You don't want to leave these to the last minute, because quality matters here—so plan them on your calendar for the week and give yourself enough time to concentrate on them in advance of the deadline. This approach will give you a heads-up on whether a task will need more than one day to accomplish, whether it has multiple steps you need to complete throughout the week, or whether you need time to gather information from other people who may not be available every day. You can't leave these tasks to the last minute, because they produce important results.

Daily planning is for your C tasks, the daily Prevent Pain things you have to do. You can plan these the night before, in the morning when you first wake up, or upon arriving at work. Whenever it works for you, take 5 minutes to plan the next 24 hours. Keep in mind all of the time-specific items on your calendar (these are your events, appointments, meetings, A tasks, and B tasks) and then think of all your time-flexible C ("have to") tasks on your to-do list for the day. Number these tasks in order of priority or how convenient it will be to get them done that day. This is your daily plan. If you have a day that is filled with time-specific events, then you'll be left with less time for time-flexible tasks. Sometimes days like this leave no time at all for flexible tasks. Being tied up in meetings for most of the day requires some recovery time in between to check e-mail and voice mail, take a break, or deal with any small fires that have come up during your last meeting. Overplanning this time in between will only leave you frustrated. A lighter day with few or no time-specific items planned will allow you to fit in more time-flexible tasks.

A key to daily planning is to do it *before* you check e-mail and voice mail for the day. If you don't, then whatever those e-mails and voice mails bring to your attention is where your productive time starts to go. A daily plan gives you more control over your productive time.

By their very nature, e-mail and voice mail are ways that other people bring what's important to *them* to *your* attention. And it's unlikely that anyone has ever become wildly successful by just doing what is on other people's agendas. When we base our planning process on what others want from us, it's hard to get out of that mind-set. Starting the day by giving away our productive time often means that we end it that way as well—and don't get to address our own important agenda. You can avoid this trap by prioritizing other people's requests of you and working them into your plan accordingly. This will keep you from spending your most valuable time on something that doesn't do anything to further your own goals.

Now, what happens if you have planned the perfect day but when you check voice mail or e-mail, you discover that an urgent matter requires your immediate attention? Perhaps it's not even that urgent but simply more important than what you had scheduled. When this happens, having the plan will help you make better decisions. A plan allows you to weigh the voice mail matter against your plan and decide on the best way to use your time. Otherwise, you're not comparing that voice mail—as compelling as it is—against anything else. When you don't have something against which to weigh your decisions, *everything* seems to be a top priority. You are, of course, ultimately in charge of what gets accomplished on your plan and what doesn't. If something more important comes up, you can change your plan to accommodate it. A plan lets you see it for what it really is and make better choices.

NO TIME TO PLAN?

People frequently say they don't even have time to plan. And it's true that taking the time to think and write things down instead of just jumping in to whatever catches your attention first requires effort and discipline. However, you'll be much more effective when running your day according to a plan—and you'll see a difference in the results you get as well. The crises and time crunches that make us overwhelmed and stressed are often created when we commit to something without writing it down. Then we forget about it, procrastinate productive time away, overcommit our available time, or get an unrealistic idea about the time it takes to do the things we have to do.

The following section will show you how spending just *5 minutes* each day making a daily plan will allow you to keep control over your productive time.

BENEFITS OF A 5-MINUTE PLAN

Benefit #1: You Don't Forget Things.

How can your brain retain a memory of climbing on a jungle gym at age four and then forget the name of the person you met 10 seconds ago? (See Figure 6.1.)

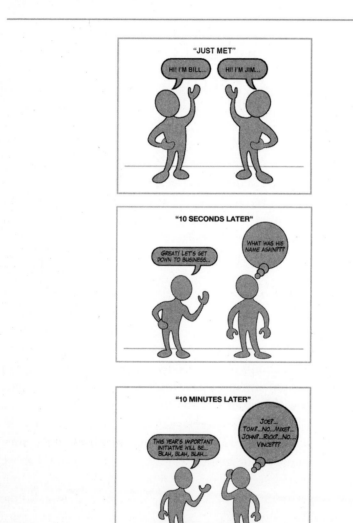

FIGURE 6.1

Our brains are funny that way. We talked in Chapter 4 about how brain chemistry is designed to help us with survival. However, if you're depending on your brain to recall a list of important things, you might want to call in some backup—just in case.

Imagine there is a new memory technology device on the market. It has the amazing ability to instantly return your attention at random times to things that you forgot to do in the past. That might be helpful, but the technology has quirks. First, you can never predict *when* it's going to work and when it isn't. Second, it's often too late to do anything about the matters it brings to your attention. Third, it can only hold one or two thoughts at a time. When you enter a new task or thought, an existing one is deleted.

How long do you think this device will last on the market? It sounds like it would cause more stress and frustration than anything else. But here's the kicker—this device is *your brain*.

This is what your brain does to you. You fall into bed after an exhausting day—and what happens as you start to drift off to sleep? Bam! Something you forgot to do last week at work pops into your head. Oh, thanks, brain! That's helpful! Not only are you *not* able to sleep peacefully; you can't do anything about that work assignment right now! How about when you get up to go into a different room and wonder the second you arrive, "Why did I come in here?" You forgot what you meant to do a mere 3 seconds earlier because you had another thought in the meantime. It's similar to the frustration you feel when you are in the middle of a sentence and you forget what you are talking about. Your brain started that sentence and then forgot what it wanted to say. And I know exactly what you're thinking when a waiter doesn't write down meal orders for a large group at your table: "Why doesn't he just write them down?! He better get them right!"

If you saw your brain on the shelf of a retail store you wouldn't buy it! Yet people rely solely on their memory to manage their lives all the time. However, there is an easier, less stressful (and perhaps more reliable) way to manage your life.

When you have a plan with a few appointments and several time-flexible Prevent Pain tasks on it, you no longer have to *remember* all those things; you only have to remember to follow your plan. In Chapter 8, we will discuss more about structuring your calendar and to-do list to maximize their effectiveness as well as different types of systems to use. And it doesn't matter what system you use; you will still enjoy the benefits of having a plan. One of these benefits is a significant reduction of stress. Your system allows you to focus on one thing at a time, keeps details from falling through the cracks, and prevents those unpleasant bedtime memory jolts.

Benefit #2: You Get More Done in Less Time.

Even people who don't normally keep a plan or a list seem to do so the week before vacation. Why? Because they know that there's no time to waste that week; every minute *counts!* If you want to fully enjoy that precious vacation time, you can't be thinking about what pain you didn't prevent before you left and what consequences will be waiting for you when you return.

Having a daily plan enables you to move from one time-flexible task to another without using too much transition time. Wondering what to do next wastes time and leaves you open to interruptions and distractions. This is when you are most likely to snack, chat, be distracted by social media, catch up on news, daydream, go get coffee, surf the Internet, and so on. These things are not as likely to throw you off your stride when you are in the middle of something specific. I'm not suggesting that you should *never* take breaks. But if you need to conserve productive time, cutting down on transition time between activities or tasks is an effective way to do that.

Following a daily plan also improves efficiency. Think about it: Who gets out of a grocery store faster, the person who goes in with a list of items separated by aisle or the person who wanders in with no list and no direction? I've done it both ways, and I'm sure you have too. If time is not an issue, go ahead and wander and enjoy it! But if time is a concern, having a plan is more efficient because it gives you direction. It makes each step easier; you can put your energy toward the tasks at hand instead of figuring out what to do next as you go.

Benefit #3: You Are Proactive, Not Reactive.

Planning in advance allows you to be proactive, and as we discussed in Chapter 4, this keeps stress and urgency low, allows for better-quality work, keeps you in control, and allows *you* to decide the best time to complete a task before the deadline decides that for you. When you don't have a plan, productive work time will elude you until the last minute. You end up being *reactive*—which brings on high stress and urgency, lower-quality work, and less control and convenience.

Being proactive also enhances organization by allowing you to group similar tasks together. Instead of going down to the first floor of your building for a meeting and then coming back to your desk afterward only to find you have to go back down to talk to someone else, you can plan in advance and save time by doing those things together. Group your meeting topics together so you can make the most out of the time you have with everyone in one room. It's the same reason why it makes sense to keep a grocery list: because running to the store every time you need one item would be a waste of time.

This is why you want to categorize questions for your boss or a client—so you don't have to interrupt a second time by calling the person back. It's also why you tackle together small jobs that require getting up from your desk, or even buy birthday gifts for a date far into the future while you're already out shopping.

Benefit #4: You Make Better Decisions.

A plan gives you a method for weighing your time's opportunity cost and negotiating the best way to use it. It also gives you a realistic idea of what you can accomplish today by accounting for your time-specific events and appointments, as well as your time-flexible tasks. And as you already know, a plan gives you something to weigh new priorities against. When you're planless, you're apt to agree to anything that comes along and requests your time. A plan lets you compare those opportunities or requests to what you already have planned and decide which choice is best for you.

For example, let's say you have to be in a meeting all morning today and might have some time in the afternoon to do an important B task and a few time-flexible C tasks. Then your boss shows up at your desk and asks you to start on a project that day. Without a plan, you might start on that request immediately—and possibly be left rushing to do your B task tomorrow before it is due and pushing off your C tasks until their deadlines as well. *But* . . . you have a plan! You can say to your boss, "Boss, I need your help. Here is my plan for the day. Is this new request more important than me attending the morning meeting? Or should we extend the deadline on my B task that's due tomorrow so I can get to this new request today? Should I push off these C tasks that you asked me to do today until another day, and do this new request instead?" Perhaps your boss will inform you that what you already have scheduled is more important than the new request. If the opposite is true, you might be able to skip the meeting to work on it—or postpone your Cs until the following day. Whatever the outcome, you have made an informed decision—*because you had a plan*. Whether you stick to your plan or abandon it in favor of something new, you can make a better decision based on what you know you can realistically accomplish. You can always readjust your plan if something urgent comes up. But you *always* need a plan in the first place.

Having a plan helps you say no to things that are poor uses of your time. And we all know that saying no can be difficult and uncomfortable sometimes. However, you say no to things all day long without realizing it. Remember the opportunity cost of your time; when you devote your time to any one activity you are in essence saying no to everything else you could be doing at that time. For instance, imagine that we are in a meeting together; by attending this meeting, you are saying no to phone calls, e-mails, other meetings, and interruptions during that time. You would also be saying no to taking the day off to play golf. Every time you say yes to one thing, you say no to everything else for that time period.

Let's say you invited me to a party this Saturday and I declined because I already have plans to go to a wedding. Would you be offended? Probably not; it would be unreasonable to be offended because I already have an important event planned for that day. I wasn't saying *no* to *you*; I simply have already said *yes* to *something else*.

What about when we *don't* have an event planned? Imagine the following conversation:

You: Hi, do you want to see a movie tonight?
Your friend: No thanks.
You: Do you already have plans?
Your friend: No.

Okay, you probably won't be calling that friend for a while. He didn't have an excuse; he just said no! You *probably* would have preferred if this had been the response:

Your friend: No, thanks, I can't. I have an early flight tomorrow. Tonight I plan to pack and get to bed early. I'll call you over the weekend when I get back; maybe we can catch up then.

This is much less likely to offend you. Staying out late at the movies when he has to get up early would be a poor use of your friend's time. Even though he did not have an important event planned for tonight, he was able to say no without offending you because he already had a plan.

Have you ever had the following kind of conversation with a friend?

Your friend: What are you doing Monday night?
You: I'm going to visit my mother. Why?
Your friend: What are you doing Tuesday night?
You: I have to work late Tuesday night. What did you have in mind?
Your friend: What are you doing Wednesday night?
You: I don't have anything scheduled Wednesday night. Why are you asking me, though?
Your friend: Great! Come over Wednesday night, and we'll watch a 3-hour documentary on bird migration patterns.

Now perhaps you *enjoy* birds *and* their migration patterns, but even if you don't, guess what you are doing Wednesday night? And you're doing it because your friend just *looked for your unplanned time*. Why? Because whatever your friend comes up with will beat *nothing* in priority—and *nothing* is what you had planned.

There certainly seems to be an unwritten rule about requesting someone's time: if they decline your request, they better have something else planned. Otherwise, you'll be offended. We respect when someone says they have time defended; we're less likely to respect undefended, unplanned time. People believe that planned time is important. But if they ask you to do something and you don't have a plan, then you should give greater priority to their suggestion—versus doing nothing. This is how we get pressured into doing things that aren't good uses of our time.

Having a plan gives you choices. You can always change it if you deem a new request for time to be a higher priority. If it isn't, having something else planned is a socially acceptable way of saying no. The key to success with this is not to get better at saying no but to get better *at saying yes to the right things*—and then letting your calendar speak for you.

Of course, it's not practical or even possible to plan 100 percent of your time. But the more positive and productive time you have planned, the fewer poor uses of it you wind up accepting because of professional or social pressures.

Benefit #5: You Can Better Recover from Interruptions.

When you are working from a plan and you are interrupted or distracted, all you have to do is refer back to your plan to resume your productivity. No matter how long this interruption takes, you can return to exactly what you were doing before it happened by referencing your plan. But when you don't have a plan in place, recovering from these interruptions is often more time-consuming than the interruption itself. Recovering well keeps your productivity on track. We discuss methods of dealing with interruptions and distractions in more detail in the next chapter.

MAKE IT A HABIT

How do we make something effortless and put it on autopilot? Make it a habit and a regular part of your routine! If you make it a habit to put your A tasks and B tasks on your calendar, then you will effectively cut down on procrastination when quality matters. Each Gain task on your calendar will bring you closer to the results that will improve your life. The way to do this is to create a habit out of planning. Then, once it becomes a habit, you won't need discipline to do it anymore.

Chapter 7 Managing Interruptions

And now, excuse me while I interrupt myself.

—Murray Walker

Now that you're armed with a plan, you can use it to keep your brain on a short leash and stay focused. But what happens when you have to deal with the interruptions and distractions that come from working with other people? Has anyone ever surprised you with an urgent request that took you so far off your plan that you never actually returned to what you were doing for the rest of the day?

It's incredibly frustrating to end a day feeling as if you made no progress on your work. After all, you were sitting right in front of it all day, weren't you? But you didn't even get through all your Prevent Pain tasks. So what happened? Occasionally—and probably more often than we'd like—the actual amount of time that you spend doing productive and focused work may be less than your optimal level.

Interruptions and distractions are inevitable in most work environments. Even people who work from home and can avoid the office atmosphere contend regularly with unplanned phone calls, e-mails, their own thoughts, mail delivery, kids, pets, and anyone else that happens to skate, run, or walk by the door during the day. Thankfully, most of these diversions are brief. I have worked in office environments that were filled with chronic work and nonwork-related distractions—including teams that routinely held meetings in open areas where everyone could hear them, a busy central printer location near my desk, and even a foosball table in the office.

But distractions are different from interruptions. Distractions can come as a result of problems with self-discipline or perhaps with office culture. They might be things going on around you that draw you away from your tasks and ruin your focus. This can become a problem if it happens too frequently; in that case, you need to set parameters about noise or perhaps change the location of your office. An overly distracting work atmosphere can lead to poor productivity and frustrated employees who think the demands placed on them are too high, unfair, or unattainable.

Interruptions, on the other hand, take place when someone wants your attention while you're trying to focus on something else. We spend so much of our time in collaborative work nowadays that we've come to accept interruptions as a natural part of our day. But some of these interruptions that take you away from your work can take over your entire day. An inability to manage these might mean you are required to take work home, or stay late after everyone else has left so you can finally get to *your* responsibilities.

People in one office where I worked constantly needed to walk up to each other's desks to ask for shared work products. How easy is it in that type of environment to start drifting away from work matters and begin discussing weekend plans? It was nice to work in a friendly environment, and I enjoyed the relationships I formed there. However, I found myself and others struggling to stay focused while worrying about being rude. I knew I had to find a way to manage interruptions when I needed to get work done.

An easy solution would be to shut your office door or put up a do not disturb sign at your desk and refuse to deal with anyone. However, this usually isn't a realistic option, because interruptions often involve work that concerns you, work you must address. Not all interruptions are superfluous office chat—and they aren't *inherently* bad. Sometimes the information or people you need can come to you at inconvenient times; you may feel interrupted, but you are still glad to have them. Sometimes helpful or even great things can come by way of interruption. However, you do eventually need to return to what you were doing before these things happened.

I tried researching articles to find out what behavioral experts advised about managing interruptions, but the tactics I read about didn't seem to work for me. The experts suggested doing things like standing up when someone approached your desk, avoiding eye contact when they inter-rupted you, or trying to go to *their* desk instead of having them come to you. One even said something about shortening the front legs of the chairs in your office so that people would feel like they were sliding forward when they sat down. This would make them uncomfortable and encour-age them not to stay as long. That advice actually made it into a *published book!* It sounded a little ridiculous to me. So I came up with my own methods of managing interruptions over time.

The questions I sought to answer were:

- How do I address the interruption (and the reason behind it) without getting off course or being rude when I am short on time?
- How do I quickly get back on track after an interruption so I don't waste *more* time?

These are the questions we will address here.

STICK TO THE WORK INVOLVED

It can be difficult to recover once an interruption gets out of control or the scope starts to drift. Whether you like the interrupter or not, you occasionally wind up wishing your phone would ring to get you out of this long unintended conversation. This is why you must establish a *time parameter* for the interruption as soon as it comes up. This is the key to keeping it brief when you need to.

The best way to do this is to state what you are doing at the moment someone approaches you—and then ask a pointed question.

Here are some examples:

"I was just trying to get through my e-mails. Is this something quick or do you want to schedule some time together for later on?"

"I have some phone calls this morning. Did you want to discuss something specific, or are we talking later?"

"I'm headed to a meeting in about 5 minutes. Can you give me the 30-second version of your problem, or do you want me to call you back when my meeting is over?"

Even a short directive such as "How can I help you?" or, for a phone call, "What had you thinking of me?" can quickly get to the reason behind the interruption and let your colleague know you don't have time for small talk today. This sets the tone and sends the message that you'll be sticking to business.

If you discover that this interruption might take awhile, then you should schedule a 15-minute appointment with this person for as soon as you finish the task you're working on. If your pointed question reveals a matter that will require more than a few minutes to address, say something like, "I'd be glad to help you with that. I have something I'm finishing up in about a half hour. Can we schedule 15 minutes then? I'll come to you." Then when you reconvene in a half hour, you can again establish time and scope parameters by saying something like, "Okay, we have about 15 minutes. Let's see if we can cover the two issues you mentioned. What do you need from me?"

The work of an interruption can usually fit into one of three categories:

1. A *task* that someone wants you to complete ("Send the project timeline to Michelle.")

2. An *appointment* someone wants you to schedule ("Can you attend a meeting with Dave and Jackie at 2:00 PM?")
3. An *exchange of information* (for example, background information or decision strategy)

If the work involves putting a task on your to-do list or adding an appointment on your calendar, then your pointed question can usually allow you to stick to the work and keep the interruption to a minute or two. However, an interruption that requires the exchange of information could take much longer—and may wind up forcing you to rearrange your afternoon.

Someone seeking an information exchange is looking for data, facts and figures, or background, context, opinion, and advice/decisions. For example, someone stops by your desk to ask about the outcome of a sales call. If you simply convey the facts of whom you met, that the sale was a success, and the amount of the contract sold, this interruption should take no longer than 2 minutes. However, providing information on the background, context, and opinion may require you to explain how you were referred to this client, why the client chose your product over a competitor's, details of the contract, and whether or not you think it will be a long-term relationship. You may have to answer, "How do you think we should proceed with this client?" If an interruption starts to move into the area of background, context, opinion, or advice, you need to turn it into a scheduled appointment because this information takes longer to communicate. An unplanned interruption is not the best setting for this type of exchange. Suggesting a meeting at a more appropriate time, preferably after you have finished your current complex task, ensures that your discussion gets the time and attention it deserves and that you don't lose focus on the work to which you have committed for the day.

STEER IT BACK BY INTERRUPTING YOURSELF

Sometimes, despite your best efforts, a brief interruption can lose direction. You can often see this coming by observing a colleague's nonverbal communication or body language; the colleague may be light on work and have time to waste. If current events, the weather, or other unrelated topics come up in discussion, a polite way to refocus the conversation without making your colleague feel slighted is to *interrupt yourself* (instead of the colleague) in midsentence. When it is your turn to talk or make a comment, stop, state your time constraint, and revisit the original work of the interruption. It would sound something like these examples:

"I know, it's the middle of December and it feels like May. We were outside this weekend too, and. . . . Ooh! I'm sorry; this contract I'm working on is due in an hour so I have to get back to it. I will send you an e-mail with the sales figures you asked for by the end of the day. It was great catching up with you."

"No, I didn't see the game last night; I'd like to try to get tickets for the game this weekend. . . . But hey, I'd better get back to this report so I can get it done by the deadline. I put your meeting on my calendar for tomorrow so I'll definitely see you then."

"Yes, I'm going to Joe's retirement party. I haven't gotten a gift yet, so maybe you can give me some suggestions at lunch. . . . But hey, I'm sorry, I've got to get these client calls done today so I better get back to them. I'll get the project status to you by tomorrow."

This technique allows you to close your conversation politely and let your colleague know that you do not have time to chat today.

SET EXPECTATIONS

If someone interrupts you with a task request, you must set a time frame for completing it. Unfortunately, it can be hard to get a straightforward answer as to when something needs to be done; the response is usually "as soon as possible." Here's a good rule of thumb: if completing this task will take less than 2 minutes, do it now. Execute the work and move on so you can get back to what you were doing before and you do not have to revisit this task again. If it will take longer than 2 minutes, then dropping everything to work on it immediately may not be the most realistic or efficient way to handle it. To avoid misunderstanding and get an accurate idea of the other person's expectations, always ask for the *latest date and time of completion* so you can work it into your plan. If you can't achieve the deadline because of your schedule or workload, you need to make that clear from the beginning. Being realistic about your time constraints can help you both prioritize what is most important and figure out in what order you should complete your work.

The goal is to get to the work of the interruption as fast as possible—thereby allowing you to preserve your productive time. There are days when you have more time for small talk and relationship building in the office. But when it's not one of those days—when you have what feels like mountains of work to do—ask a pointed question, stick to the work involved, and set expectations so you can get back to work.

RECOVER AND GET BACK TO WORK!

So you've managed that interruption and successfully turned your attention back to your scheduled work. Now . . . *what* were you doing again?

A great deal of research has been done on the loss of productivity associated with interruptions, and the recovery time needed—especially regarding how much this productivity loss ends up costing corporations. A 2008 study concluded that interruptions cost US corporations $680 billion in lost productivity annually, and other studies have reported that a typical office worker spends almost a third of his or her day dealing with interruptions and the associated recovery time.[1,2] (See Figure 7.1.) Research also emphasizes that the more detailed and complex the task you are doing when you are interrupted, the longer recovery time you'll need to return to the same state of concentration you were in before the interruption occurred.

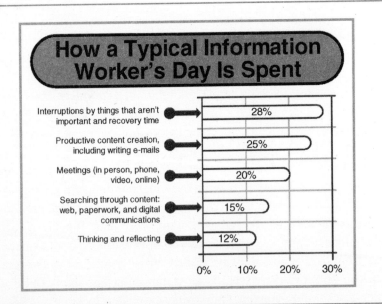

FIGURE 7.1

This is the most crucial time to refer back to your written plan—because one of its benefits is telling you exactly *why* you don't have time to chat today. By consulting your plan, you can return to your scheduled projects and goals for the day and get back to productivity more quickly after you've addressed the interruption. If you are working on a detailed, tedious, or complex part of a project, then you can help yourself recover more efficiently by recording where you are on your plan when you get interrupted. You should also note what your next action should be when you return to working on it, because you usually can't depend on your brain to remember a relevant thought you just had. Make your note as detailed as possible to provide a mental cue to trigger the state you were in when you left off so you can refocus. I even do this if I'm working on a continuing project at the end of a workday; it allows me to jump in the next day more easily and not torture myself trying to remember a great idea I had just before I left off the previous day. In essence, I treat the end of the workday as an "interruption" to the flow of work that I was doing so I can resume without wasting time the next morning.

Figure 7.2 shows a summary of these interruption management strategies.

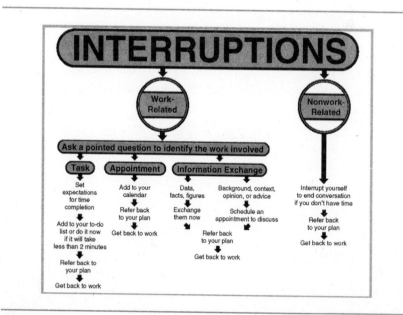

FIGURE 7.2

WORK INTERRUPTIONS INTO AND OUT OF YOUR SCHEDULE

Of course, some projects require more concentration than others; therefore, you might need to schedule an appointment with yourself and make it a time during which you are *unavailable to be interrupted*. If you have the flexibility, this includes letting calls go through to voice mail, not checking e-mail, putting a sign up at your desk that you are unavailable from 10:00 to 11:00 AM today, or perhaps even moving to a conference room or other quiet location where you can close the door. If you work with a team that shares electronic calendars, you can add this appointment so everyone knows not to disturb you. Conversely, you could schedule a block of time when you are available for interruptions or open door time when you welcome requests and are available to answer questions.

RETURN THE FAVOR

Last, remember to follow all of these suggestions when *you* are the interrupter. Tell the other person how long you will need, get right to the work of the interruption, and clearly negotiate your expectations for time completion if appropriate. Then, let the person get back to work. If you need more than a few minutes of someone's time, send a meeting request with a few highlights of what you need to discuss. Ask the person to schedule some time for you when he or she reaches a stopping point. This way you don't interrupt the person's concentration. If you are direct and brief, then you won't make your colleagues feel as though they have to hide the next time they see you coming down the hall!

Chapter 8 How to Manage It All
Time Management Implementation

Organizing is what you do before you do something, so that when you do it, it's not all mixed up.

—A.A. Milne

Now that you've decided what Gain activities would bring significant results in your life and have committed to prioritizing and planning accordingly, as well as keeping up with all your "have to" obligations, you might be wondering, "How do I manage it all?"

Do you remember back in your academic life, when you had a separate notebook for each school subject? When it was time for math, you took out your math notebook. You knew exactly which one it was because you had written "Math" on the cover, and your notes from your last math class were right there! We color-coded everything: red for math, blue for science, yellow for history, and so on. That's what back-to-school was all about: deciding where your stuff was going to be for that year so that you could easily find it when you needed it. We were so brilliant back then, weren't we? Most of us were more organized with our important information at age 11 than we are now. Today, many people are more likely to be in this situation:

> "Where are your notes from last week's meeting?"
> "Ooohh . . . umm . . . it was a yellow pad. . . . I doodled a tree in the corner. Look for the tree."

How's that for a retrieval system? (Your schoolteachers would be disappointed.)

Being organized simply *makes things easier*—to find, to remember, and to manage. It also *saves time*. Time management is all about organizing and systemizing your information resources, which is what you're going to learn to do in this chapter.

ORGANIZING YOUR INFORMATION RESOURCES

To be in control of your responsibilities and your time, you must be in control of your information resources. These include your:

- To-do list (tasks)
- Calendar (appointments)
- Contacts
- Notes

If you can keep these resources organized and under control, you will be able to:

- Keep your commitments to other people.
- Remember and keep all your appointments (including your Gain tasks).
- Pick up where you left off with clients and colleagues.
- Organize all your information so that you can reference it easily and save time looking for important information.

Some people struggle with these things throughout their whole lives. Their tasks and contacts are everywhere, on sticky notes, napkins, or the back of a business card. (See Figure 8.1.)

If you don't have systems in place for managing these things, you probably tend to rely on floating pieces of paper or sticky notes to remind you of important commitments or information. You may have several different calendars that have conflicting obligations. You may not know how to retrieve information that you took the time to gather at some point

FIGURE 8.1

in the past. This type of "I hope I don't lose it" strategy is likely to cause stress when you inevitably *do* lose or forget something and wind up missing a commitment. Having a system that can organize and simplify your information resources will save you time and frustration. It also helps when it comes to time management, and the following sections will cover exactly how to do this.

WHY GET ORGANIZED?

You can think of having a time management system as a way of *uncluttering* your mind just as you would attempt to unclutter your home. For example, think of a small item in your home that is the least likely thing to ever be lost, such as eating utensils: forks, knives, and spoons. Do you ever hear anyone in your home say, "I'd like to eat now, but I have to look around for a fork and spoon. Has anyone seen them lying around?" I don't know of *any* home that doesn't have a place where these things are regularly kept. The cycle of use for these items—between being in the drawer, being used, being cleaned, and being returned to the drawer—is so basic that if someone found a random fork on the bathroom countertop or under the couch, it would be immediately apparent that it was out of place and it would be returned to the kitchen without any thought. As a result, we never have to spend time looking for these things, and there is no such thing as fork and spoon stress! Have you ever said to anyone, "How's it going?" and the person's answer was, "Dude, things are so bad, we don't even know where the forks are." Oh, man; that's *bad*.

Wouldn't it be great if there were more things in your life that were this easy to keep track of? In your home or office, physical items need an assigned location in order to be found and used repeatedly. If no location is assigned to an item where it belongs when it's not in use, it becomes *clutter*. And not only does clutter cause a messy space, but it also causes stress.

A few of the ways that disorganization causes stress are:

1. You can't find an item when you need it, which makes you frustrated.

(continued)

(*continued*)

2. Items are constantly lying around and getting in the way. You have to move them from place to place when you don't need them, which causes extra work for you.

3. Cluttered space makes you feel like you always have unfinished work to do, prompting anxiety and draining productivity.

4. Sometimes you will buy more of something because you simply can't find the one you had, which means an extra expense.

Be honest: Do you have something on your dining room table right now that doesn't belong there? Did you think to yourself when you bought that item, "The dining room table would be the perfect place for this"? Of course not. You probably weren't thinking about where you would keep it. But until you decide where that item belongs, you put it in random places. It then becomes clutter that causes stress every time you look *at* it or look *for* it. If you can't find an item when you need it, it cannot be useful to you. Once you assign a (preferably out-of-the-way) location to it, *then* it can be useful to you. You know where it is when you need it, thereby eliminating a hassle. This is how being organized reduces stress and saves time.

Clutter and messiness can also incite embarrassment or shame in many people. Most of us don't want to appear to be disorganized or out of control. Have you ever noticed that the amount of disorganization in our physical space usually translates, at least to some degree, to the amount of control we feel over life at any given time? How do you feel when your physical space is clean and neat, with everything in its place? Even if other things in life are causing you discomfort or grief, at least your *space* is not one of them. We draw comfort and peace from an organized, relaxing space; it allows us to be more creative, productive, and clearheaded than a cluttered, disorganized space. How do you feel when your space is cluttered and messy and you have trouble finding things? You're likely frustrated, anxious, stressed, depressed, tired, and out of control— emotions that *drain* creativity and productivity. Simply cleaning up and organizing a space can help alleviate these negative emotions, reduce stress, and give you a boost of endorphins and pride from which you can gain energy, as we discussed in Chapter 4.

The simple difference between feeling stress and not feeling stress in some areas of your life, such as organization, comes down to *making a decision*. For example, you have *decided* and *committed* to the fork and spoon system in your house. The system works, and you don't need to make any further decisions on that topic. You *haven't* yet made a decision about the items on your dining room table. You haven't committed to a system.

This is also true for your information resources, which is what makes all of this relevant to time management implementation.

> **Just as you need to organize your physical belongings to remain in control of your physical space, you also need to organize your information resources to maintain control of your responsibilities and your time.**

In the same way that you decide and commit to a location for items in your home, you must also decide and commit to one location or system to organize your to-do list, calendar, contacts, and notes in order to reduce the stress of managing your responsibilities and time. This allows for greater peace of mind and productivity.

DECIDE AND COMMIT

As usual, the hardest part is the decision. Psychologists cite the most stressful life events as the death of a loved one, a change in jobs, and a move from one home to another. What do these events have in common? It's decision, decision, decision. . . . You have to make so many decisions in a short period of time. Have you ever visited someone a year after he moved and he's not settled yet? Try asking him, "Hey, what's in that box over there?" Your friend is probably thinking, "I don't want to talk about that box!" Why not? What do you think is in the box? *Decisions* are in the box! What are you going to do with this? How about that? Do you even need this anymore? Should you donate this? You have to make a decision about *everything* in the box!

Decisions can be difficult, because they make our brains work hard. This is illustrated well by a lab study done on rats. Scientists put a rat in a maze with a piece of chocolate at the end. The rat could smell the chocolate as soon as it was released into the maze, and its brain activity started going crazy. It searched and corrected its course throughout the maze until it found the chocolate. They repeated the experiment daily, and the rat exhibited less brain activity each day while following the correct path to the chocolate. As the rat learned and repeated the activity, it needed to search less actively. Instead, it followed a memorized path to the reward, which meant that it no longer had to work hard and make decisions about the best way to find it. Its brain activity returned to a baseline level.[1]

Sadly, humans aren't all that different from rats (at least in this instance). We have to be fully engaged in what we are doing when we are learning a new activity and making decisions. It requires attention, focus, and analysis; we can't be multitasking and thinking about other things. Once we make a decision, learn the system, and make it a habit, our brain's autopilot takes over. We don't have to be as engaged in the task and can even think about other things while we are doing it.

We do this sort of thing anytime we turn decisions into habits. Think about the first night you lived in your current home. You moved in and started to settle your belongings in the new space. What happened when it came time to put your keys down? You probably took an extra few seconds to think about where you were putting them to ensure you would be able to find them in the morning. Some people put a hook near the door to hang them; others have a small dish in the kitchen or the foyer for their keys. Some people have them in their pocket all day and put them on their nightstand at night only to return them right back to their pocket in the morning. Whatever you do, you know that this is an *important item*—something that, if lost, will definitely cost you some time. So you make a decision to place your keys somewhere every night, and you don't have to think about it after that. You *created a habit*.

If you choose and commit to a system for managing your to-do list, calendar, contacts, and notes and turn it into a habit, it will become a *nondecision system*. This will reduce stress, save time, and ensure that you don't forget appointments, overcommit, lose information, or miss deadlines. Once this is a habit, you will no longer have to stop, think, and decide how to handle new information. How would you like to be *that* organized?

The best solution is to develop and then *use* an integrated system that includes the ability to collectively manage all of these resources. The challenge is not finding such a system; many are available. It's *committing* to effectively using the system you've chosen. If you can do this, you will reap the benefits that come with this sense of control, such as remembering things, feeling more organized and less stressed, finding things more quickly, and managing your day more efficiently.

THE KEYS TO USING A TIME MANAGEMENT SYSTEM EFFECTIVELY

Regardless of which system you choose, committing to it requires that you follow two major rules:

1. **You must use your system *exclusively*.** Commit to only *one* location for your tasks, appointments, contacts, and notes. Put time-flexible tasks (both personal and professional) on your to-do list, and put all time-specific appointments (personal and professional) on your *(one!)* calendar. Put all contacts (personal and professional) in your contacts list, and categorize all notes into a single system where you can most easily access them. We will discuss how to use each of these resources effectively in the coming sections. For now, keep in mind that using only one system for both work and personal commitments is a must. Keeping separate to-do lists and calendars for work and personal matters leads to overcommitting because you can't be in two places at once.

    An important part of this step is *to get rid of all floating pieces of paper.* In other words, don't write yourself a sticky note as a reminder to call someone; put the reminder in your task management system. Don't shove reminder notes in your pocket or text yourself about an appointment; put those on your calendar right away. Don't keep a notice about a late bill on your desk or print out all your e-mails to remind you about tasks or meetings. Put all of this in your system, and let *that* be in charge of remembering important things for you. If you have tasks and reminders on sticky notes everywhere around your office, home, and car, then you will never know if you have kept track of everything. I've even seen plenty of people put sticky notes on their computers! How ironic is that? It's the one thing that could store information the most efficiently, yet people ignore its most helpful function and put a sticky note on it. It's not just sticky notes; it's notices reminding you to do something, files left on your desk until you are ready to deal with them, and so on. This is how you lose track of obligations. Tasks that are written down on floating pieces of paper are like items on the dining room table; they clutter your mind until you can get them done. Just like the forks, tasks need a system. Using one system exclusively ensures that nothing will be lost or forgotten.

2. **You must keep your system with you always or have mobile accessibility to it.** You have to be able to access your system from both your home and office computer or remotely from a mobile device such as a smartphone. What typically happens if you can't access your system? When someone asks if you can make it to a meeting this afternoon, you will have to respond, "I'll check when I get back to my office and shoot you an e-mail." If someone asks if you can go out to lunch today, you will have to say, "Let me see how my morning goes, and I'll give you a buzz later." Shooting and buzzing! That's not being in control; that's creating more work for yourself.

   Having constant access to your system—in your office, at home, or from your mobile device—will keep you in control of your responsibilities and time. You will always know where you have to be and what you have to do. Sounds pretty basic, doesn't it? The truth is that almost everyone struggles, at least some of the time, with being late, missing appointments, forgetting or delaying tasks, overcommitting your time, double-booking, or running out of time. You can conquer uncertainty and avoid these slipups by having one system and keeping it with you always.

WHAT YOUR SYSTEM NEEDS TO DO

Technologies will change, and new tools, apps, systems, or smartphones will come to the market to help you manage your information resources. Extra features and bells and whistles can be helpful, convenient, and even fun, but whatever system you choose, it must help you do three basic things:

1. Create daily and future to-do lists (in other words, give each task a date).
2. View time-specific and time-flexible obligations *at the same time* (appointments and tasks for the day).
3. Document categories of information (keep contacts and notes).

Most technology-based systems and smartphones allow you to do all of these things. The most helpful—yet probably least utilized—feature is the ability to view your calendar (time-specific) and task list (time-flexible) for each day at the same time. To optimally manage your day, you need to see both where you have to be and what you have to do together.

Let's look at each one of the information resources to see how best to manage them and why they are essential to your time management system.

TASK MANAGEMENT SYSTEM: TO-DO LISTS

Let's say that someone says to you, "Give me a call in about three weeks to follow up," after a meeting or project. How do you keep track of that task? Do you put it on your calendar as a time-specific appointment even though it has no specific day or time assigned to it? Do you write it on a to-do list and let it sit there for three weeks? Do you put a sticky note about it on your office wall?

As you might have guessed, none of these are the ideal approach. But if you systemize tasks, they come to you when they are supposed to be done. Then you can remember, prioritize, and execute them.

Systemizing simply means storing tasks according to the date you can complete them. You must put every task that comes your way on a daily or future to-do list. Managing these lists is your task management system. Let's look at how these lists work for you.

As we know, time-flexible Prevent Pain tasks don't go on your calendar; they go on your to-do list. Remember the keys to using your system effectively: use only one system, get rid of floating pieces of paper, and always be able to access your system.

Keeping all of your tasks together will ensure that you always know what you have to do. You simply check your list to make sure you haven't forgotten anything. This reduces stress, gives you peace of mind, and makes you feel confident in your ability to follow through on your "have to" obligations as well as your "don't have to" (*but want to*) Gain tasks.

Your task management system should give you the ability to create a daily to-do list and future to-do lists.

Most people have a rolling to-do list that just goes on and on from one day to the next. Every time they think of something they have to do, they add it on. Then they wind up looking at every task that is on their mind, every day, regardless of whether or not they can actually accomplish it that day. (See Figure 8.2.) Do you think this makes it more or less likely that you'll actually complete that day's pressing tasks? *Less* likely, of course. Not only is looking at everything, all at the same time, that you have ever thought of doing overwhelming, but it's unrealistic to even consider trying to complete all of that.

FIGURE 8.2

You wind up adding to your list on Monday, adding a little more on Tuesday and Wednesday, hoping you lose it by Thursday, and throwing it across the room by Friday.

Systemizing tasks eliminates this sense of frustration. It requires that you store your tasks according to the date they can get done.

Consider a day like what's shown in Figure 8.3.

When you have a day like this, where time-specific appointments are taking up the majority of the day, your flexible time is limited. It's unrealistic to try to fit in everything you have to do. You will wind up feeling anxious and frustrated that you didn't accomplish what you'd set out to. If you do this day after day, tasks accumulate on your list over time.

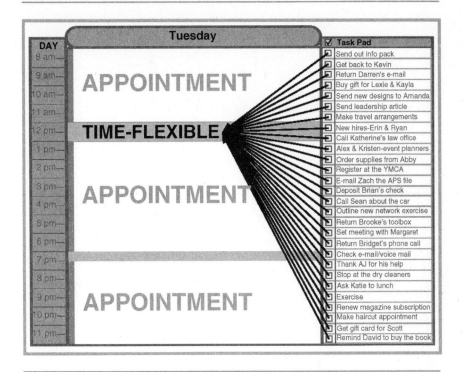

FIGURE 8.3

After a while, you become numb to their presence, and you never actually complete them until they become urgent. This bad habit allows only the urgent tasks to catch your attention. Other tasks fall through the cracks, and you forget about them. This is the reactive model of motivation by fear that we discussed in Chapter 4. The rule for creating a manageable daily to-do list is this:

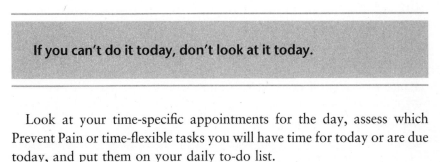

If you can't do it today, don't look at it today.

Look at your time-specific appointments for the day, assess which Prevent Pain or time-flexible tasks you will have time for today or are due today, and put them on your daily to-do list.

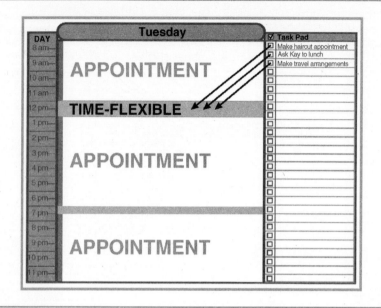

FIGURE 8.4

Figure 8.4 shows a more appropriate list for a day like this. You can take advantage of the small amount of productive time in between your appointments by scheduling just a few Prevent Pain tasks. It's far better than overwhelming yourself with a long list that is impossible to attack on a day like this. Just as you did when you were scheduling your Gain tasks in Chapter 5, look at your time-specific commitments when you are creating your daily list, which should include the Gain tasks you put on your calendar. Then see how many of your Prevent Pain tasks you can fit into the remaining time-flexible space. If you're looking at a reasonable list instead of an overwhelming one, you are less likely to waste time and more likely to actually accomplish your tasks. You will also be less likely to scrap your Gain task appointment for less important Prevent Pain tasks.

You should schedule everything else for a day when you have a better chance of getting it done. If you know you can't do a task until next Wednesday, put it on next Wednesday's to-do list and don't let it stress you out today. Then when you take your 5 minutes to plan that Wednesday, you will see that task. This is what a *future* to-do list is for.

Here are some examples of tasks that would go on a future to-do list:

1. Ellen requests that you call her to follow up on a project in three weeks. Add the task "call Ellen to follow up on the XYZ project" to your task list and give it a date of three weeks from now. This will keep you from looking at that task on your list every day until then. When that date arrives, there it is; you can complete it then, without thinking about it in between. You could also make a time-specific appointment to call her on that day, thereby making that task an appointment on your calendar. But if you don't assign a time to it, it is on your to-do list for that day three weeks from now.

2. You want to remember to pick up a gift for Dave's fortieth birthday, but you don't have time to do it today. Add "get Dave's birthday gift" to your task list for a specific date when you will have time to accomplish it so you don't show up at the party empty-handed.

3. You have a product due to a client in three months, and you have delegated steps to Jay to complete along the way. Add "check with Jay on progress of step 1" to a date two weeks from now. Add "check with Jay on progress of step 2" four weeks from now. Add "check with Jay on progress of step 3" six weeks from now.

4. You have a sales call with a client who says he is not ready to buy yet but you should check back in a few months. Add "contact Brett to repropose" to a date three months from now.

5. Every year you think to yourself, "Why did I wait until the last minute to make dinner reservations for Mother's Day?" Add "make Mother's Day reservations" to your task list for a date in December or January (or as early as you wish) so you are sure to make Mom happy and get into the restaurant of your choice on that special day in May!

6. You have a project with eight steps. Use your task list to plan out the steps so you can be sure to stay on track. Add "step 1," "step 2," and so on, to your task list for the dates on which you need to complete them.

7. You have a client who places an order roughly every three months. Add "check with Peter about reordering" to your task list every three months just to make sure he isn't considering going with the competition.

Creating a future to-do list relieves stress and allows for realistic planning. It allows you to only look at the tasks that you actually have time for on a given day. If you can't do it today, you don't look at it today. Put it on your list for whenever you will be able to do it. This is a 365-day to-do list or, as I call it, a future to-do list. If you do this, you can forget about a task on purpose until you are ready to do it, at which point it will come to you.

You might be wondering about the difference between a 365-day to-do list (a future to-do list) and a calendar. Your calendar is for time-specific appointments with other people, or appointments you have with yourself to accomplish your A tasks and B tasks (your Gain tasks or your important documented Prevent Pain tasks). Your 365-day to-do list is for your time-flexible Prevent Pain tasks that eventually have to get done. Future to-do lists make sure details and commitments don't fall through the cracks. If it goes on today's to-do list, you should be able to do it today. If you can't, put it on a future to-do list and forget about it today.

This is where you'll experience another benefit of using a technology-based system. Once you have given a task a date, your device will remind you of the task on that day. Many e-mail systems can be set up to sync with your mobile device and have a reminder pop up on your phone on the date you indicate. You can also have it backed up on your hard drive. This makes your system a daily and future to-do list at the same time. It also allows your system to automatically move any item you don't finish on a given day to the next day. Some systems even turn them red or otherwise remind you that they are overdue.

This approach allows you to follow up with tasks you've assigned to others, too. If you have delegated a task to me that was previously your responsibility, you can choose a follow-up date on your future to-do list to ask about the status of the task. This approach is also the key to contact management. If you check in with your clients or team members at different intervals, you can use this to keep track of your next obligations without having to make a time-specific appointment with them.

Future to-do lists also prevent you from feeling overwhelmed by a never-ending list of tasks. They eliminate that sense that you failed to accomplish all of them at the end of every day. The purpose of all this is to balance the number of tasks that we have to do and the time it will take to do those tasks with the amount of time that we are not in time-specific appointments that day. Balancing tasks and appointments is the key to not feeling stressed and overwhelmed. On a day when you have appointments all day, you should have two or three tasks at the most on your to-do list. If you try to do more, you feel overwhelmed and your productivity and energy is lower. And who did this to you? That's right, your parents. *They* did this to you. Always blame your parents! Just kidding. *You* did this to you, because you were unrealistic about your constraints.

To recap, you will want to use the following for your task management system:

1. Decide on *one location* where you will list all your tasks, both personal and professional. The best option is a technology-based system that you can access from your mobile device and have with you always. You also want to make sure it's backed up remotely on your computer or online in case you lose your mobile device.
2. Commit to using *only your chosen system* so that you always know where to look to see what you have to do. This means you must *stop* using all other reminder strategies, including floating pieces of paper.
3. *Divide your task list* into daily and future to-do lists by giving each task that comes your way a date by which you want to accomplish it. This gives you a separate to-do list for each day. Be realistic about your constraints each day to reduce stress and take advantage of the productive time you have. If you can't do it today, don't look at it today. Put it on a future to-do list.

CALENDAR

What is your current system for keeping track of appointments? How would you remember the date if someone invited you to a barbeque next month? Would you put it on your kitchen wall calendar at home? Would you put it on the calendar in your smartphone? How about your calendar at work? Would you have to do all three?

Having two separate calendars for personal and professional commitments doesn't give you two 24-hour days at the same time; it just gives you a headache when you realize you've scheduled conflicting commitments. All your appointments need to be in one location. You can't separate them because you can't be in two separate places at once. Do you have friends who constantly say yes to things without checking or putting it on a calendar? They're the ones who end up cancelling later because they've committed to something else, haven't worked it into their day, or have simply forgotten what they said yes to. Using a calendar effectively prevents this.

There is an old saying: "A man who has a watch always knows what time it is. A man who has two is never quite sure." The same is true with your appointments. Having two places where you keep commitments almost guarantees an eventual scheduling conflict, whereas having one ensures that you always know where you are supposed to be.

The keys to using your calendar effectively are the same as the keys to using your task management system:

1. Decide and commit to *one calendar system* for all personal and professional time-specific commitments.
2. Have it with you always or have mobile accessibility to it.

Some people keep something called a communication calendar. This may be a general calendar for an entire department at work so that everyone knows where a team member is that day, or it may be one for the family at home. These can be either online or posted on a paper wall calendar. The key is that this calendar is for other people who need to know where you are at a given time. This is not meant to be your sole reminder of a commitment. Every appointment that you have on that communication calendar also needs to be on *your* calendar so you can see all your commitments at the same time.

Having mobile accessibility to your calendar is also crucial. This lets you immediately decide whether to accept meeting requests, invitations, or other commitments without having to check your calendar at home or work.

You already know that your calendar also includes the appointments you make with yourself to pursue your Gain tasks. In that way, a calendar represents where we spend our time and therefore what we value. We express that we value certain pursuits and relationships by *giving* them our time—our most precious and irreplaceable resource.

THEY WORK TOGETHER

We explained in the previous section on to-do lists that you need to check your calendar for time-specific obligations before making your daily to-do list. This keeps you from scheduling too many tasks in an insufficient amount of time, thereby setting yourself up for failure.

But what happens when your to-do list is your top priority for the day? Occasionally, you become so heavily burdened that there's no time to schedule *any* time-specific appointments that day. This might be the case if you have items with a due date approaching, or you have been waiting patiently on a future to-do list for so long that you must consider these tasks when making new appointments for the day. Let's say, for example, you're planning a big event. The few days leading up to it are probably not a good time to make appointments for new clients or pursuits. You will likely be burdened with errands, details, tasks, and last-minute preparations. And although these don't necessarily have times assigned to them, you must nonetheless complete them sometime before the event. On days like this, your to-do list may be your highest priority. You need to complete the items on it to ensure that your event is successful, so scheduling time-specific appointments for other things will have to wait.

Your calendar and to-do items must work in conjunction with each other because both represent commitments or responsibilities that you have. You have to consider both when planning your day.

This is why you must use a system that lets you see your daily time-specific and time-flexible obligations at the same time. If you see your future to-do list on a given day is full of many "have to" tasks that will prevent pain from coming your way, then that clearly won't be the best day to schedule a maintenance meeting with the budget department or to schedule lunch with a client. Even though nothing may be time-specific, you still have a lot to accomplish that day. Conversely, you may be able to fit in only one or two time-flexible tasks on a day with back-to-back meetings.

You can make good decisions on how to best spend your days only if you *make a habit* out of planning. Knowing what is ahead of you—and when you have time to give your attention to it—is a skill that you develop from habitual planning and prioritizing. And it's one that your calendar system will help you develop by allowing you to:

- Plan your Gain tasks on your calendar and *defend the time* to do them.
- Use *only one calendar* for both personal and professional commitments.
- *Consider both* your time-specific and time-flexible tasks on any given day when planning and prioritizing.
- Use a system that gives you *mobile accessibility* to your calendar from your office, home, or wherever you are so you can always make good decisions about your time and commitments.

BEING ON TIME VERSUS BEING LATE

We know that time is precious and valued—our own, as well as other people's. We also know how important being on time is. The purpose of keeping a calendar is knowing where you are supposed to be. However, just *knowing* where you need to be at any given time doesn't guarantee that you will be there!

The simple truth is that people who are chronically late for obligations don't have problems managing time; they have problems managing decisions *to be on time or not*. The underlying issue is the choice to fulfill your commitments and recognizing—rather than ignoring—time constraints. And mostly, it's about respect. If you respect your commitments and the people to whom you make them, including yourself, you will want to be on time for them and you will find a way to make that happen.

Think about it this way: if I offered you $1 million to be on time for a morning meeting, no matter how early it started, you would be there, right? You would make *sure* you were not 1 minute late. In fact, I would venture to say that you would probably be early just so you could anticipate any obstacles to getting there, such as traffic, train or subway trouble, alarm clock malfunctions, and so on. You would probably double- and triple-check the time and place of the meeting. Some people might even get a hotel room the night before right next to the meeting location and set three different alarms for the morning. (I mean, we're talking about $1 million here!)

If the commitment is important enough to you, you would be able to find a way to fulfill it, no matter what. All it takes is a little thought, planning, and common sense to know what might stand in your way and to determine how to handle it. So what does this say about a commitment that you are late for? It says that the commitment is *not important enough for you to be on time*. It also tells the person or people you're meeting that they're not important enough to you either.

People who are habitually late make lots of excuses. What all these excuses truly say is they don't respect the commitment or *the relationship with the other person* enough to be on time.

This is what those who show up on time and then have to wait will learn about the latecomer:

1. This person does not respect our relationship.
2. This person does not respect his or her commitments.
3. I cannot count on this person to be reliable.

Their sense of trust with that person is broken. Conversely, each time a commitment is honored, trust is strengthened and respect is conveyed.

There are always exceptions, of course. There are instances when you can plan all you want, leave early enough to get somewhere with time to spare, and still be set back hours by a traffic jam. Sometimes anything from a sick child to a flat tire or a late train can come up unexpectedly and upset your well-thought-out plan. If the person you have kept waiting in these cases is unaware of your predicament, he or she will usually assume that you are being rude or disrespectful. But because these situations have happened to everyone, usually a sincere apology and explanation of what happened is all you can offer to remedy the situation. And it's typically enough to dispel any feelings of disrespect if you are genuine and did the best you could to let the person know as soon as possible that you would be late.

It's important to respect a relationship, in *any* area of your life, because it affects how much and whether people trust you. If you repeatedly damage trust with another person, it will be difficult to recover. Perhaps you never realized what it says about you when you fail to follow through on commitments.

That being said, there are some situations when being late is more acceptable than others. For example, a large gathering with many attendees, such as a party, has a start time on an invitation. But most social circles accept a certain window of time, such as the first hour of the gathering, during which everyone will arrive without being considered late. On the other hand, planning to meet a friend at a restaurant for dinner at a certain time is a different situation. If you were an hour late in this case, you would have an angry friend to whom you owe an apology.

Business commitments will *always* fall into the second category. When you have made a time commitment to call or meet someone or to arrive at a meeting of *any* size, you must respect the time of all other participants. Everyone involved has made a time commitment; if they show up on time and you don't, they have learned that they cannot trust that you will do what you say you will do. They may have also learned that you value their time less than your own. Having this reputation in business can reflect negatively on you in many ways. It can keep you from winning proposals, from being chosen for a project team, from being promoted, and from being able to gain others' cooperation when you need it.

Do you know anyone with a reputation for being chronically late? Is this the type of person you would trust with a large contract for your business? I don't think so. *So don't be that person.* Understand that the commitments that you keep say a lot about how trustworthy and reliable you are, and the commitments that you don't keep say just as much. Show your respect for your relationships by keeping the commitments that you make to the people in your life and your business.

INFORMATION MANAGEMENT: CONTACTS AND NOTES

Managing your important information is a crucial part of your time management system because it is a matter of convenience, time savings, and organization. How many times during your day or week do you have to reach out to other people for your business? How often do you have to remember when you spoke to someone, what you talked about, and what you are supposed to do before you speak to that person next? How many times do you reach for the same reference material each week? Having this information in an organized system can save you from wasted time, frustration, or even embarrassment.

Contact Management

How do you keep track of the people in your life and your business? Do you do this only for personal contacts, or do you have extensive client files? These questions bring us to the next information resource. Keeping track of the people in your business and your life is called contact management. So, what is your current contact management system?

This doesn't just entail phone numbers, addresses, e-mails, and other ways to reach people. It also includes files on your past dealings with them, your recent touch points, and pertinent personal information such as a spouse's name, a favorite spot for a lunch meeting, or the past contracts or projects that you have had with this person. This type of contact management is crucial in occupations such as sales or professional services, or really in any occupation in which you have regular or repeated client contact.

Many companies have elaborate contact management systems and train their employees on how to manage these important relationships. But even if you don't have a system like this, you still need to keep track of the people with whom you do business, whether they are clients, colleagues in your own company or industry, or networking acquaintances.

Many e-mail systems and mobile devices allow you to have a file or page for each contact that includes space for making notes on the last time you spoke with the person. As with your to-do lists and calendar, the best way to manage your contacts is to decide on *one location* for all personal and professional contacts and commit to using is *exclusively*.

Having one system for your contacts ensures that you don't lose important contact information and that you always know where to look for it when you need to retrieve it. As with your to-do lists and calendars, you must keep it where you can always access it or be able to access your system from your mobile device.

If your mobile device is your primary system for contact management, be sure to back it up on your computer or online regularly in case you lose your device. Losing this information would be detrimental to your business, and it would take too much time to rebuild.

Notes

Where do you take notes? In meetings? On client calls? In workshops? How about lists? Do you have lists for the grocery store, weekend home projects, local restaurants? As with your other information resources (I think you know what's coming here!), you must decide and commit to *one location for all of your notes*. You then can keep any information that you find yourself repeatedly referencing in a central location, making it faster for you to retrieve. For instance, if you attend weekly meetings where you take notes, then you might just need a low-cost paper notebook that can reside in your desk since this is probably not something you will need to have with you all the time. Notes may not be as vitally necessary to keep with you always as your other information resources are. Of course, if you do need to access your notes or files remotely, then technology-based notes applications are the way to go.

Most people categorize notes according to the *contact or person* they pertain to (as in a contact management system for sales), *the date* they were taken (as in weekly meeting notes), or *the topic* they pertain to (as in a multifaceted project). Decide which classification is most appropriate for you, and commit to it so you can easily find your notes when you need them. If you need to access your notes pertaining to ongoing projects remotely, you'll want to use technology-based files.

Whether you choose technology-based notes and lists or paper files, keep each category of notes in one location. If you cannot reference them when you do need them, then it's futile to take them in the first place.

TOUCH IT ONCE

There is one more rule that will help you be more productive once you have your systems for managing your information resources in place: *touch it once*. This simply means, make a decision when something is front of you. For example, have you ever opened an e-mail or received a phone call asking for something and thought, "Oh no, that is going to take me 20 minutes. I don't have time to do that now"? Did you just skip it and go on to the next e-mail? Did you write a sticky note? You already decided that the time to do that task is *not* now. Just take it a step further and decide, "If not now, when?" Once you decide, put it on your future to-do list for that day and don't worry about that e-mail or voice mail message getting buried and forgotten. If it is an appointment, then enter it on your calendar right away so you don't forget to do it later. Training yourself to take small steps the moment a task or new piece of information appears will eventually make it a habit.

If you can make it a habit to be organized with your to-do lists, calendar, contacts, notes, and other important information, you will be able to maintain control over your responsibilities, your time, and your results. How does that sound? Peaceful? Stress-free? Productive? Even triumphant? It is something else too . . . it is completely *achievable* if you decide and commit to a time management system that incorporates Gain as well as Prevent Pain into your daily plan.

Chapter 9 Take Action

Do you want to know who you are? Don't ask. Act! Action will delineate and define you.

—Thomas Jefferson

THE POWER OF YOUR DECISIONS

We started out talking about motivation and Gain, balance, priorities, energy, and the importance of valuing time. We also discussed practical ways to use planning and organization to maximize time and productivity in order to achieve the results that would improve your business and your life. Can just improving the way you make decisions *really* impact all of that?

In a word, yes. The decisions that we make result in the life that we build. The life you have today is the cumulative result of all the decisions and circumstances that have been part of it up until now. Some of these circumstances—where you were born, who your parents are, the health of your family members—are completely out of your control. But the decisions you make as to how to handle the situations that life gives you, what risks you take, what you spend your time on, and the Gain you decide to pursue are what makes you different from everyone else. These are the things that *define you*.

Part of what makes your decisions critical to building your life is that every decision has consequences, whether intended or unintended. These are the ripple effects of your decisions that can be far reaching through all areas of your life or layers of your organization. When you are young, having choices is a sign of growing up and being trusted with responsibility. In that way, it is a cherished privilege. As we grow up, our parents teach us about consequences by letting us make increasingly important choices about things we can control, such as what to wear, what to order on a menu, whom to date, and which extracurricular activities to participate in. The consequences gradually become more serious for each decision we make—for instance, when we decide which career to choose, whom to marry, and what values to embrace in our behaviors. We even take on decisions that affect other people, such as our family members or employees. It is then that making decisions goes from being a privilege to more of a responsibility. All the consequences that come from a decision, even the unintended ones, are yours to live with and take responsibility for. You cannot blame them on or credit them to anyone else. They too become part of who you are.

DECISIONS ARE LIKE RULES

Remember when you were young and you would join a group of kids outside to play a game in the neighborhood? The first thing that everyone had to establish was the rules. So many things in life work the same way. Sports would be nothing without the rules of the game. Office cultures, families, sets of friends, and social organizations all have rules that are made known, whether they are spoken or unspoken. Whether or not everyone adheres to them determines how well the group's members get along and how many problems there are among them. Learning the rules makes it easier for everyone to know what to expect in a given situation.

However, these are all rules made up by other people. You may not always think they are fair.

In your own life, *you* get to make up the rules. We might not call them rules, but have you made any decisions that you will live by and would never compromise? These are frequently guided by ethical principles or just by life experience. They vary widely, from "I will never buy anything on credit that I don't already have the money to pay for," to "I will never take advantage of someone else to get ahead." These absolutes are also a part of who you are. It may not always be easy to live up to them, especially if you have set high standards for yourself. However, once you have decided that you want an absolute to be a part of your life, it takes away a decision point and thereby simplifies things. Just as in physical space organization and information resource organization, once you make a decision or a rule like this—whether in your personal or professional life—you no longer have to think, analyze, debate, wonder, or spend time on it. You know what to do when the situation arises. And knowing your rules helps guide you toward decisions or actions that would make you happy.

YOUR DECISIONS DETERMINE WHO YOU ARE

Sometime around the early 1970s, someone came up with the notion of "finding yourself." This term became a generational mantra, used as justification for everything from engaging in risky behaviors, to ending relationships, to taking off to foreign countries with little more than a backpack and a rebellious attitude. I'm not completely sure if the term had the same meaning to everyone who used it, but I *am* sure that it confused a lot of people who heard it. How does one lose oneself to the point where one has to go to distant lands to then find oneself? And how do these risky behaviors and distant travels solve the problem? Countless lost souls—as well as naïve, dramatic soap opera and movie characters—were left globetrotting and soul searching trying to find themselves or figure out who they are for decades due to this cruel conundrum. I think it's time to help them out!

Knowing who you are means knowing *how you are different from everyone else*. What makes you an individual? In other words, what do you do that you don't have to do? What do you believe in enough to pursue on your own even if you don't have to do it? What makes life worth living for you? The time to answer this usually comes a little after you stop wanting to fit in all the time and begin wanting to stand out from the crowd a little because of your talents, skills, character, or competence. Regardless of how you search, the answers aren't out there somewhere. All you have to do is consider some different questions that only you can answer:

- What do you value?
- What are the absolutes in your life?
- How do you want your life to be?
- What do you want to accomplish or experience?
- What would make your life better than it is today?
- What are you going to do about it?
- What do you want people to think or feel when they hear your name?
- What do you want people to remember you for?

If you can answer these questions, then congratulations; you have found yourself! You can go home now, because you already know who you are.

But most people have never thought about these questions or they don't know the answers. They're confused by this concept of figuring out who they are because they're stuck in a rut, checking off items on their "have to" list every day. They don't understand where their self-identity comes from because they are busy doing the minimum requirements of life, and they are burned out from it. They are putting almost all of their efforts into merely *surviving*—which is what they see everyone else doing too—and they don't understand what makes them different or what makes someone an effective leader. If you have answered or are working toward answering these questions and you decide and commit to pursue Gain in your life, then you are unlikely to wind up in this situation. But *you* are the only one who can answer them. As we discussed in Chapter 1, you are the only one who can identify the Gain that would make your life better, end burnout and bring balance, escape a rut, relieve depression, and infuse energy into your pursuits. Only you can put yourself on the path to leadership, a path worthy of travel and one that inspires others both personally and professionally to follow.

DO YOU MAKE LEADERSHIP DECISIONS?

Your decisions and their consequences determine who you are—and whether or not you are a leader. Whether they result in leadership, management, or mismanagement, they are what define you. If your decisions move things forward and improve the situations around you, then you are a leader. If your decisions lack the courage, ingenuity, vision, or effort to make any sort of improvements, then perhaps you have been a good manager; that is, you have been adept at keeping things the way they are and maintaining the status quo but not necessarily at enhancing anything. If you've made your decisions based on ego or emotions such as resentment, envy, or selfishness, then perhaps you have mismanaged your responsibilities and left things worse off than they were before.

Business leadership is about forging new paths and moving an organization forward from where it is today, rather than keeping things the way they are. Similarly, *personal* leadership is about leading your own life in the direction you want it to go, rather than following other people's ideas of what your life should be. In business and in life, Gain does that for you. It's hard to identify what makes you unique if all you do every day is fulfill Prevent Pain tasks like everyone else—showing up for work, taking out the trash, and paying the bills. What do you do that's unique from anyone else? What have you improved? What have you created? What have you done that you didn't have to do? Your Gain tasks are what distinguish you from other people. Pursuing Gain and making improvements is leading— yourself *and* others. These are the activities that will prevent burnout, make your efforts worthwhile, bring satisfaction and balance, and generate the momentum to keep you going.

IT'S NOT A COMPETITION

You are building your identity when you are working toward Gain. Your identity comes from knowing who you are, what you have accomplished, and where you are going. So how will you get your identity if you don't have any movement in your life? How will you differentiate yourself? Too many people try to garner this sense of self from the outside world, namely, by competing with and sizing up against others. This is the approach people take when their egos are threatened or unsatisfied because it's your ego's job to protect and validate you. Without the strong sense of self-identity that comes from pursuing Gain, your ego will try to compensate by competing with and comparing you to people around you.

Chances are, you've had a conversation with someone who does this. If your company had 10 percent growth, this person's had 20 percent and opened two new offices this year. If you just went to a concert, this person had front row seats at another one. If it snowed 1 foot at your house, it snowed 2 feet at this person's house last winter!

It can happen in the oddest of circumstances. My mother-in-law was holding my infant son at a party a few years ago and remarked to the woman next to her, "Doesn't he have the chubbiest little legs?" The woman immediately came back with, "My grandson's legs are twice as chubby as that!" My mother-in-law brought the baby over to us laughing and told us to feed him more because she just lost a chubby baby contest! We didn't even know there was a contest going on, but apparently, we had entered and lost!

Those people are identifying themselves as part of a category. They then separate themselves from others in the category by making themselves superior. This competition gives them the identity of being a winner at something. You can feel the competition unfold as the conversation goes on if their ego is threatened.

It goes something like this:

You: My daughter plays soccer.
Other person: My daughter plays soccer, too. *(Identify.)* She plays in a select league and she was MVP this season. *(Separate and make superior.)*
You: This is my favorite band.
Other person: Mine, too. *(Identify.)* I've been a fan of theirs for 20 years. I had backstage passes to their first concert tour. *(Separate and make superior.)*

You: My aunt is sick.
Other person: My aunt was sick. *(Identify.)* She was my favorite. *(Separate.)* She just died and left me lots of money. *(Make superior.)*
You: I used to play on a baseball team.
Other person: I used to play on a baseball team, too. *(Identify.)* In fact, my team went to the state championship *(Separate.)*, and I scored the winning home run! *(Make superior.)*

Perhaps all these things are true. These people might *really have* more global offices, more snow, more soccer goals, and chubbier babies than you do. But the tendency to turn every conversation into a competition comes from a lack of self-identity, a lack of satisfaction with their lives, and a failure to understand who they are and what makes them unique. They are trying to establish and develop their identity using *external* measures (the people around them) instead of building themselves up from the *inside*.

This lack of identity doesn't just cause people to *compete* with others; after a while, they actually start to *root against* others, because they don't feel good about where their lives are. This is inevitable because if you compete *all the time*, you can't *always* win. They watch the news every night so they can see the horrible messes other people have made of their lives. They then turn off the TV and go to bed feeling better because they're thinking, "Well I had a bad day, but it wasn't as bad as that!" Their identity comes from knowing that some other people are worse off than they are. The best thing these people can say is, "At least I'm not on the 11:00 news!"

Sadly, people don't just do this with strangers on TV. Being stuck in a rut can negatively affect your personal relationships as well. For example, let's say that you and I are friends. Your life is moving forward and improving month after month, and mine is standing still or getting worse. After a while, I start to feel envious. The competition and resentment set in, and now I secretly want you to *trip* in that marathon you're doing this weekend! I am actually rooting against you, because I don't want your life to be improving when mine isn't.

When the ego takes over and I start to root against you, it becomes difficult for the relationship to succeed. After all, relationships are about connecting and understanding, not separating and competing. Competition implies that there is a winner and a loser, and there can be no winner in a relationship. Anyone who sees himself or herself as a loser in a relationship will suffer from damaged self-esteem and encounter problems, such as allowing other people to manipulate or take advantage of him or her. If, on the other hand, you're constantly trying to win, you're likely to obsess over how others perceive you. You'll become overly concerned about what your status is in regard to material possessions, such as cars and houses, or titles and positions in business or society. Your relationships will deteriorate in either case, because trying to beat everyone at something is exhausting, not to mention damaging. It erodes the trust that two people need to have to be in a successful relationship, whether that connection is professional, a friendship, with family, with neighbors, with team members, or with someone else.

If competition and envy have compromised your relationships and the best thing you can say about your own life is, "At least I'm not on the 11:00 news!" then it's probably time to insert some Gain into your life. Gain can help restore balance for one incredibly significant reason:

Pursuing Gain returns the focus inward.

Once you have decided to work toward Gain, you change your focus. You concentrate on *you* and *your goals* and *what you want to experience* instead of what other people think or are doing. In short, you end the competition.

BUILDING YOUR IDENTITY AS A LEADER

Working toward Gain builds identity and self-esteem, because your creation goals in particular define you and build your legacy as a leader. You can't build an identity by only pursuing consumption goals; these are an *escape* from life and responsibilities. You use them as a *reward* for the work that you do. You also can't build an identity by doing your laundry or taking out the trash or even by showing up for work every day. Doing what you have to do to get by is just doing your job and preventing pain. It's expected, and it won't bring any movement to your life.

To make something a part of who you are, you must go above and beyond what is expected. You must be passionate enough about something in life to do more than the bare minimum required. That passion is what breeds authenticity and builds identity.

Pretty soon, you'll be finished reading this book. You should then go back to the end of Chapter 1, where you initially brainstormed your list of goals. Now make your list again in light of the things in life that you are passionate about. Think about *growing* your business or career, *strengthening* your important relationships, making the things you love a bigger part of your life—anything that helps you experience movement. Think about making things better, because that's what leaders do. The same passion that is necessary to lead your own life is necessary for leading an organization, department, or team. The person who can pursue their own goals and values is worthy of being followed by others, just as someone who cannot do this likely *lacks* the ability to effectively lead others.

To live without goals is to live without passion for anything, and that will only lead to burnout. Working toward creation is what ends the burnout and the competition.

If you are pursuing Gain, you won't resent or envy other people's goals or movement; you'll be too focused on your own journey. Detrimental emotions such as competition, resentment, or envy will be replaced by the energy and sense of accomplishment we discussed in Chapter 4. Your relationships are actually apt to *improve*, because you will not feel the need to root against other people; you'll be too focused on rooting *for* yourself. Once you are *leading* your own life instead of just *managing* it, you will be able to lead your relationships better as well. You will be able to celebrate other people's accomplishments and growth, because you will be secure with who you are and where you are going.

DON'T JUST THINK ABOUT IT. *DO IT!*

Your goals are not a part of who you are until you do something about them. They are merely *intentions* until they are on your calendar. The calendar is the force that will compel you to act on them and work toward the results they will produce. The calendar is the simple tool we need to begin making our intentions a reality.

This need not—and often *doesn't*—happen fast. Most things that are worthwhile do take some time to accomplish, after all. Is there just one thought in the back of your mind that you are working on? Take it just one goal at a time; that's completely fine. Think about it today, then *do* something about it today. Get it on your calendar, and continue acting on it from there tomorrow. Before you know it you will be on your way to achieving it, and what would your life look like then? Better than it does today, I'll bet. And that's what Gain is about!

Do you know people who have mismanaged their lives to the point that they hate everything about them? Do they feel trapped in cycles of unhappy work situations, crushing debt, dysfunctional relationships, and even health problems that stress has caused or exacerbated? People in this situation feel everything is a "have to." They say things like, "I'm not in charge of my life!" or "I need a paycheck!" or "I don't have any choices!" They feel that they have no control. Burnout and stress are running their lives and they are at a low point of motivation and productivity.

But even those starting from this discouraged state have choices and can turn things around. I have seen individuals like this make progress and work toward improving their lives when they take responsibility for the choices that got them there and decide and commit to pursue Gain.

Consider anything at all. It could be the smallest short-term goal that can improve your life, even something seemingly insignificant like organizing your office. Then schedule a small consumption goal for when you've finished that. Say, "I'll organize this office so that I can stop losing everything, then I'll go out and take a walk with a friend during lunch." Or, "I'm going to learn how to use that new computer program tonight so that I can make my job a little easier; then I'll relax and watch a movie before bed." Being in control of that one little thing will make you want to seek *more* control. So schedule time among your Prevent Pain tasks to improve something else tomorrow, and then the next day, and so on. You will eventually see a shift, a way out of the rut, even just by starting with the smallest goal.

Time will continue to move forward and your life will happen whether you plan it, direct it, consider the consequences of your decisions, or not. How will you decide what to do when important choices come up? When you have identified goals and absolutes that you want to be a part of your life, you will be able to focus on where you want to go. And knowing where you want to go will help you make decisions and choose paths that will get you there.

There are things you *have to* do in life and things you *don't have to* do. As it happens, the most important and enjoyable things—such as happiness, accomplishment, improvement, and leadership—are all on the *don't have to* list. No one will hold you responsible for them. You have to *want* them, work for them, and earn them in order to get them. Having a good balance in your life between the "have to" and the "don't have to"— between Gain and Prevent Pain—is the way to end each day feeling balanced and satisfied with your effort. And of course, this requires that you shift your priorities toward results.

YOU WORK TOO HARD NOT TO GET THE GREAT RESULTS YOU DESERVE

There always seem to be questions lingering: When is it due? Who do I owe it to? What will happen if I don't do it? The answers to these predominantly determine how people decide to use their time. The problem is that these questions are *other*-focused. They leave *you*, and what you want to do, completely out of the equation. Have you ever heard someone order from a menu at a restaurant and think, "With all these great choices, he picked *that*? I never would have picked that!" Other people frequently don't make the same choices we would make in any given situation. They will most definitely not make the same choices you would make for your career or your future. If you leave your time in their hands and use these other-focused questions as the criteria for your decisions, you will surely prevent pain, but that's *all* you will do. You may never get to what you want to do.

We don't experience the best life has to offer for us as individuals when we are constantly other-focused to the point of suppressing our own identity. We quickly become tired of thinking about what other people want us to do, what they need us to do, what we have to do, what we have gotten ourselves into, and what we have to do to get ourselves out of it. What happens if that is all we think about for a decade? Burnout, midlife crisis, depression, and rut are some very unpleasant possibilities.

If all you're doing is Prevent Pain tasks, you will end the week in the same place you started, week after week. Don't you deserve better results than that?

You work too hard to just prevent pain day after day. Your efforts are too great to be left at the end of the week, month, or *year* exactly where you were before. You work too hard to not experience the significant results and movement that come from Gain. You work too hard to make decisions that don't yield better results for your life and your future. You *deserve* those results, and to see the Gain in your life instead of simply preventing pain day after day.

If we can change our criteria and prioritize for results instead of for deadlines, we can start to move toward and experience the results that come from Gain. Will we still have to pay our bills and complete our Prevent Pain tasks? Sure. But when we finish the week having worked that hard, we will have a little movement, a little improvement, and a little progress toward a better life. That's what satisfaction with your efforts is all about.

Once you're better able to prioritize your decisions and your actions, the results that you are getting will improve. If you can move your life forward a little bit each week, you will begin to feel balanced. You can start *leading* instead of just *managing*.

Be the inspiration—for yourself and for others. Be the person others look at and wonder, "How do I get my life to be like that?" And then tell them how! Decide and commit to Gain, balance, prioritize, plan, and get energy from desire instead of from fear. Dedicate yourself to getting organized, getting significant results from your time and effort, leading instead of just managing, improving instead of just maintaining, and moving forward instead of standing still.

Do it for yourself *and* for the people around you because the best thing you can do for the people in your life is make good decisions that ensure you don't end up in a Prevent Pain rut.

Everyone has to make the same decision every day: "How am I going to spend my allotted 24 hours and get the most out of it?" So decide! Decide what to spend your time on based on the results it will produce. *Decide* to move your life forward!

Finishing this book is your Gain task for the day. You *didn't have to* do it, but I hope you're glad you did. I wish you lots of luck and success in whatever Gain you decide to pursue.

Now, don't forget to take out the trash!

Notes

CHAPTER 2 IT'S ALL UP TO YOU: AVOID BURNOUT AND CREATE BALANCE

1. YWCA, "Beauty at Any Cost, a YWCA Report on the Consequences of America's Beauty Obsession on Women & Girls," Washington DC, August 2008.
2. M.D. Hurd, P. Martorell, A. Delavande, K.J. Mullen, and K.M. Langa, "Monetary Costs of Dementia in the United States," *New England Journal of Medicine* 368, no. 14 (2013): 1326–1334.
3. Walter F. Stewart, Judith A. Ricci, Elsbeth Chee, Steven R. Hahn, and David Morganstein, "Cost of Lost Productive Work Time among US Workers with Depression," *Journal of the American Medical Association* 289, no. 23 (2003).
4. Teresa Amabile and Steven Kramer, *The Progress Principle* (Boston: Harvard Business Review Press, 2011).

CHAPTER 4 ENERGY AND MOTIVATION: DECIDE HOW YOU WILL GET YOURS

1. Jeroen Nawijn, Miquelle A. Marchand, Ruut Veenhoven, and Ad J. Vingerhoets, "Vacationers Happier, But Most Not Happier after a Holiday," *Applied Research in Quality of Life* 5, no. 1 (2010).
2. Elaine D. Eaker, Joan Pinsky, and William P. Castelli, "Myocardial Infarction and Coronary Death among Women: Psychosocial Predictors from a 20 Year Follow-Up of Women in the Framingham Study," *American Journal of Epidemiology* 135, no. 8 (1992).

CHAPTER 7 MANAGING INTERRUPTIONS

1. Jonathon B. Spira and Joshua Feintuch, "The Cost of Not Paying Attention: How Interruptions Impact Knowledge Worker Productivity," Basex, Inc., 2005.
2. Simone Stumpf, Margaret Burnett, Thomas G. Dietterich, Kevin Johnsrude, and Jonathan Herlocker, "Recovery from Interruptions: Knowledge Workers' Strategies, Failures and Envisioned Solutions," Oregon State University Technical Report #cs05–10–03.

CHAPTER 8 HOW TO MANAGE IT ALL: TIME MANAGEMENT IMPLEMENTATION

1. C.A. Thorn, H. Atallah, M. Howe, and A.M. Graybiel, "Differential Dynamics of Activity Changes in Dorsolateral and Dorsomedial Striatal Loops During Learning," McGovern Institute for Brain Research, Massachusetts Institute of Technology, June 2010.

Acknowledgments

Many people made this project possible and manageable from beginning to end.

Thank you to Adrianna Johnson from John Wiley & Sons, Inc., for "discovering" me in the *Wall Street Journal* and getting us started on this journey, and for believing in my message and ability.

Thank you to Sean Melvin for helping us connect the dots and giving some early direction.

Thank you to Cynthia Zigmund for your expertise and advice.

Thank you to Carolyn Monaco and Alicia Simons of Monaco & Associates for your marketing expertise, your commitment to the success of *Decide*, and your friendship.

Thank you to my nephew, Jay McClatchy, for your brilliance, talent, long hours, hard work, loyalty, support, and never-ending patience.

Thank you to Anna Drummey, PhD, for your subject matter expertise and advice.

Thank you to Christine Moore from John Wiley & Sons, Inc., for your skills in editing and your support and encouragement.

Thank you to Matt Holt from John Wiley & Sons, Inc., for deciding to take on this project and for pulling it all together.

Thank you to Erin Van Belle for your support, patience, cheerleading, integrity, and friendship. Your expert administrative and crisis management skills are second to none.

Thank you to Lindsay Durfee and PR/PR for your promotion of my ideas in the print media world.

Thank you to David Hartmann and Scott Ulrich of D2S Designs for the great interpretation of our stick figure art and pencil-drawn charts. Your talent and vision are remarkable.

To my wife, ghostwriter, and partner in business and in life, Lynn Shableski McClatchy, thank you for your wholehearted support of this project from the beginning, for your long months of writing and research, for your tireless pursuit of excellence, and for your gift of putting my ideas into words. No words could ever capture what you mean to me. Thank you for deciding to spend your life with me and for being the heart and soul of our family.

To my children: Grace, Amy, Kyle, and Kelly, thank you for your curiosity about this project, your eagerness to celebrate the milestones with me, your support and encouragement, and your unwavering trust that everything I do is for you. I love you beyond words.

To my mother, Kay, and my late father, Jay McClatchy, thank you for a childhood that could never be duplicated, a home that was filled with life, family bonds that can never be broken, lessons that will never be forgotten, a work ethic that will always serve me well, a faith that will never be shaken, the example of unconditional love that has shaped my life, and your support and prayers since the beginning. Most of all, thanks for not stopping at 10.

To my mother-in-law, Jackie Shableski, thank you for your support and prayers and for your dedication to having our family not skip a beat during this writing process. Without your help we could never have undertaken this project or made it to soccer practice on time. Words cannot express the gratitude we have for how you have enriched our family. We are beyond the point where we could ever return your kindness, and as I have said before, we can only promise to pay it forward to our grandchildren in the future.

To my family and friends, especially: MaryKate and Bill; Sally and Ted; Joe and MaryPat; Tom; Michael and Christine; Jim and Nan; John; Billy; Elisa; Rick and Cindy; Vince and Beth; Ellen; Michelle and Sid; David and MaryKay; Sally and Brett; Sam and Sally; Bob and Nancy; Peter and Suzanne; Lisa; Max; Steve and Michelle; Chris and Michele; Pat and Liz; Jay, Jack, Caroline, Tom, Liz, and Katie; Paul and Gerry; Greg and Debbie; Artie and Lisa; Raz and Julie; and Jerry and Shannon. Thank you for sharing in our challenges, labors, and excitement as this project progressed. Thank you for believing in me and for providing encouragement along the way. Our lives have been enriched by your friendship and companionship. Lynn and I are proud and blessed to call you all both our family and our friends.

About Alleer Training and Consulting's Work with Clients

Alleer Training and Consulting is a world-class training and speaking organization offering keynote speeches and partial- and full-day presentations in the areas of leadership, time management, communication skills, conflict resolution, and consultative selling.

Please visit www.alleer.com to check out Alleer's impressive client list, testimonials, keynote speaking video, and training programs or to register for the next open enrollment presentation.

To see how Alleer can be a resource for your training and development needs please contact us:

info@alleer.com
610–407–4092
Follow Steve on Twitter: @stevemcclatchy.

INTRODUCING THE NEW *DECIDE* KEYNOTE!

What shapes leaders' outcomes, career, and life? Their decisions. The criteria we all use for making decisions drive our performance—and our effectiveness as leaders. Great decision-making habits yield a lifetime of achievements and success. Poor habits keep us stressed, frustrated, and forever out of balance.

Decide shows leaders and aspiring leaders at every level we have more control than we often realize over our work and life and discusses how to make the decisions that move us forward in both. It gives people the tools they need to:

• Focus on results and the true drivers of performance.
• Regain critical planning and personal time.
• Dramatically increase work and life engagement.

This keynote is highly energizing, packed with humor, insight, and passion, and consistently results in measurable improvements in performance and productivity, higher workplace satisfaction, and greater employee engagement.

To learn more about speaking opportunities with Steve, visit www.Alleer.com or call 610–407–4092.

About the Author

Steve McClatchy grew up in the greater Philadelphia area as the eleventh of 12 children in his family. He credits his fascination with time management to his big family and lively, yet sometimes chaotic, childhood home. He attended college in Washington, DC, and holds a BA in economics and a BA in finance.

Steve comes from a sales background and has been in the talent development industry since 1996. In 2001 he started his own speaking and training company, Alleer Training and Consulting. Alleer comes from the Latin word *alere*, which means "to develop a person." He speaks, trains, and consults to many Fortune 1000 companies internationally on the topics of time management, leadership, and sales. He is a member of the National Speakers Association, the Society for Human Resource Management, and the American Society for Training and Development.

Steve serves as a guest lecturer at many of America's top business schools, including the Harvard Business School, the Wharton School of the University of Pennsylvania, Drexel University, Temple University,

Saint Joseph's University, Villanova University, the University of Chicago, and Western University in Canada.

Steve has been quoted in such distinguished business publications as the *Wall Street Journal, Entrepreneur* magazine, *Investor's Business Daily, WebMD* magazine, *Selling Power* magazine, and *Fast Company* magazine.

Steve has been a part of the Big Brother program for 25 years and has donated a portion of the profits from this book to the Big Brothers Big Sisters of America.

Steve resides in Malvern, Pennsylvania, with his wife, Lynn, and their four children.

Index